The Big Book of Sports Insults

David Milsted

WEIDENFELD & NICOLSON

Weidenfeld & Nicolson
Wellington House, 125 Strand, London WC2R 0BB

First published 2004

A CIP record for this book is available from the British
Library

ISBN 0-304-36684-6

Design by www.carrstudio.co.uk

Printed and bound in Great Britain by Clays Ltd,
St Ives plc

www.orionbooks.co.uk

Contents

Picture Credits

Prologue

'Bodily Exercise Profiteth Little'

Bodily exercise profiteth little.

The Bible, Timothy 4:8.

I have never taken any exercise, except for sleeping and resting, and I never intend to take any. Exercise is loathsome.

Mark Twain.

Exercise is bunk. If you are healthy you don't need it; if you are ill, you shouldn't take it.

Henry Ford.

Whenever I feel like exercise I lie down until the feeling passes.

Robert Hutchins.

I get my exercise acting as a pallbearer to my friends who exercise.

Chauncy Depew, US lawyer.

I believe every human life has a finite number of heart-beats. I don't intend to waste any of mine running around doing exercises.

Neil Armstrong, lunar astronaut.

I bought all those Jane Fonda videos.
I love to sit and eat cookies and watch 'em.
Dolly Parton.

At what time does the dissipation of energy begin?
Lord Kelvin, British physicist, to his wife, who was planning an afternoon walk.

One reason to smile is that every seven minutes
of every day, someone in an aerobics class pulls
a hamstring.
Internet joke, which must have originated somewhere.

Jogging | Wankers in tracksuits

Joggers are basically neurotic, bony, smug types who could bore the paint off a DC-10. It is a scientifically proven fact that having to sit through a three-minute conversation between two joggers will cause your IQ to drop 13 points.
Rick Reilly in *Sports Illustrated*, 1992.

Exactly how intricate a sport is jogging? You were two years old. You ran after the cat. You pretty much had it mastered.
Rick Reilly in *Sports Illustrated*, 1992.

The only reason I would take up jogging is so that I could hear heavy breathing again.
Erma Brombeck.

The trouble with jogging is that by the time you realize you're not in shape for it, it's too far to walk back.
Franklin Jones.

Jogging is for people who aren't intelligent enough to watch Breakfast TV.
Victoria Wood, *Thingummy Doodah*, 1991.

I don't jog. If I die I want to be sick.
Abe Lemmons, US baseball coach.

Football?

Bloody Hell!

Football causeth fighting, brawling, contention, quarrel-picking, murder, homicide, and a great effusion of blood, as daily experience teaches.

Philip Stubbes, 17th-century pamphleteer – and clearly an early observer of Millwall FC.

Football is all very well as a game for rough girls, but is hardly suitable for delicate boys.

Oscar Wilde, playwright.

My mother told me when I was 14 that football was a cruel and vindictive sport run by people with no standards. She was right.

Darren Beckford, former £1m Heart of Midlothian player, February 1998, by which time he was working as a milkman.

Football? Bloody hell!!

Alex Ferguson, May 1998, after Manchester United had scored twice in the dying minutes of the European Cup final to defeat Bayern Munich.

What a footling game it is, with its aimless to-ing and fro-ing and its nil–all draws and its narcissistic superstars collapsing in Hollywood histrionics at the merest whack on the shins … Soccer was devised to keep the drongos away from proper sports.

Mike Carlton, Australian broadcaster, quoted on smh.com.au, 2002.

The fans 50,000 idiots

Do you hear that sound? That's the simultaneous breathing of 50,000 idiots.
From Peter Terson's play *Zigger Zagger* (1967); spoken by a policeman to an arrested fan under the main stand.

The truth is this: for alarming chunks of an average day, I am a moron.
Nick Hornby, on his obsessiveness as a football fan, in *Fever Pitch* (1992).

Near the end of another football season of spitting, punching, diving, cheating, roasting, bragging, assaulting, effing and blinding and various other sporting pastimes like financial skulduggery and forgetting to pee in bottles, can I make a suggestion? Next season can we make it an offence punishable by a long prison sentence to use the description 'The Beautiful Game'?
Michael Parkinson in the *Daily Telegraph*, 3 May 2004.

The rest of the world loves soccer. Surely we must be missing something … Uh, isn't that what the Russians told us about communism?
Jim Murray, US sportswriter, in the *Los Angeles Times*, 1967.

2:0 Globalized girlies v. British blokes

**Football is a gentleman's game played by hooligans
and rugby a hooligan's game played by gentlemen.**
Unidentified chancellor of Cambridge University,
19th century.

**Footballers are globalized girlies; rugby players are
British blokes.**
Brian Appleyard in *The Sunday Times*, 23 November 2003,
after England's victory in the rugby World Cup.

■ FOOTBALLERS
a pampered set of preening prats

Reacting to a report that brain cells are damaged by heading the ball:

I don't think heading the ball has got anything to do with it. Footballers are stupid enough anyway.

Premier League spokesman, 1995.

Football has sold out. First the big game went international and then the players became a pampered set of preening prats.

Bryan Appleyard in *The Sunday Times*, 23 November 2003.

Footballers are only interested in drinking, clothes, and the size of their willies.

Karren Brady, managing director of Birmingham City, 1994.

If you are looking for a sport involving dumb animals, try Premiership football.

Martin Kelner in the *Guardian*, 22 March 2004.

Tony Adams

Eeee-yore! Eeee-yore! Eeee-yore!

Chanted by opposition fans every time the Arsenal defender (nicknamed 'donkey') hoofed the ball upfield.

It took a lot of bottle for Tony to own up.

Ian Wright salutes his team-mate as he owns up to his drinking problem.

One triple vodka,
There's only one triple vodka.

To the tune of Los Tres Paraguayos' 1970s hit 'Guantanamera',
Middlesbrough fans help Adams with his alcohol problem.

A man who's fulfilled every schoolboy's dream. He's won the Double, captained England and driven a car into a brick wall at very high speed.

Sanjeev Bhaskar introduces Tony Adams on The Kumars at No 42,
'Quotes of the Year', www.telegraph.co.uk, 30 December 2003.

Lorenzo Amoruso

Somebody compared him to Billy McNeil, but I don't remember Billy being crap.

Tommy Docherty on Rangers' Italian forward, May 2000.

Darren Anderton

Old Sicknote should get a part on Animal Hospital.

Former Tottenham star Jimmy Greaves, 1998.

Nicolas Anelka

Chim Chimeney, chim chimeney,
  Chim chim cheroo,
Who needs Anelka when we've got Kanu?

Sung by Arsenal fans after the volatile Frenchman left Highbury in 1999.

Nick Barmby

Why do people keep signing Nick Barmby?

Jimmy Greaves, quoted in the *Sunday Herald*, 2003.

John Barnes

John Barnes's problem is that he gets injured appearing on *A Question of Sport*.

Tommy Docherty, 1993.

Fabien Barthez

Like a woman on her wedding day – nervous, out of position and hoping everything would soon be over so she could go up to the bedroom.

Hugo Gatti, a reporter on the Spanish newspaper paper *Marca*, assesses Fabien Barthez's performance for Manchester United against Real Madrid, 2003; quoted on bbc.co.uk, December 2003.

Peter Beardsley

Peter Beardsley is the only person who, when he appears on TV, causes daleks to hide behind the sofa.

Nick Hancock on *They Think It's All Over*, BBC TV, 1995.

If George had been born ugly, he probably would have played till he was 40 – just look at Peter Beardsley.

Former Northern Ireland footballer Paddy Crerand on George Best, in the week Beardsley signed a contract with Australian club Melbourne Knights, February 2000.

David Beckham

This Gaultier-saronged, Posh-Spiced, Cooled Britannia, look-at-me, what-a-lad, loadsamoney, sex-and-shopping, fame-schooled, daytime-TV, over-coiffed twerp ...

The *Daily Telegraph* on Beckham's sending-off against Argentina in the 1998 World Cup.

David Beckham can be my private English teacher.

An irony-free Ronaldo on his new team-mate at Real Madrid; quoted on bbc.co.uk, July 2003.

Posh 'n' Becks — Celebrity coupling

Posh Spice is pregnant. At least that's one time David Beckham has stayed on long enough.
Bradley Walsh, *The National Lottery Show*, 1998. The allusion is to Beckham's sending-off against Argentina in 1998.

They are precisely the kind of people that one would dread as neighbours. They have lots of money but no class.
Dame Barbara Cartland on the prospect of having the Beckhams as neighbours, 1999.

Without being too harsh on David, he cost us the match.
Beckham's England colleague Ian Wright points the finger, 1998.

I don't think he's a great player. He can't kick with his left foot, he doesn't score many goals, he can't head a ball and he can't tackle. Apart from that he's all right.
George Best's verdict, January 2000.

A grossly overrated player, a speechless fop with legs as bandy as a northern jockey's.
Willie Donaldson in *I'm Leaving You Simon, You Disgust Me* (2003).

If I walked down the street with a hankie on my head and wearing a Tahitian skirt, people would point at me and laugh.

Jimmy Greaves, 2000. Greavsie never spoke a truer word.

Do ya think I'm Becksy?

Chant sung by Manchester United fans during a Champions League game with Juventus at Old Trafford, 19 February 2003, punning on Rod Stewart's 'Do Ya' Think I'm Sexy', quoted in the *Guardian*, 20 February 2003. Beckham was at the time sporting a cut eyebrow, legacy of a dressing-room incident following an FA Cup defeat by Arsenal the previous weekend, in which an angry Sir Alex Ferguson had kicked a boot which flew across the dressing-room and struck Beckham.

Becks hasn't changed since I've known him – he's always been a flash Cockney git.

Ryan Giggs, 'Quotes of the Year', www.telegraph.co.uk, 30 December 2003.

His superstardom is rooted in two things: crosses and dead balls.

David Mellor in the *Evening Standard*, 18 June 2004.

The queen of preen.

The *Sun*, 19 June 2004.

Captain invisible.

bbc.co.uk sums up Beckham's performances in Euro 2004.

Played three, blown three.

Ian Chadband on Beckham's record in major championships; in the *Evening Standard*, 25 June 2004.

You're a text machine!

Ron Manager (Paul Whitehouse) to David Beckham, BBC TV, July 2004.

If Beckham wants another tattoo, he could have on his forehead 'Not as good as Zizou'.

Simon Barnes in *The Times*, 15 June 2004. Beckham's second-half penalty miss was a contributing factor in England's 2–1 defeat by France in the opening group match of Euro 2004. 'Zizou' is, of course, Zinedine Zidane, who scored goals with a free kick and a penalty in extra time.

They have a cookery 'O' Level between them, yet their antics have dominated the media for 20 years and counting. They were made for each other, but sudden death prevented them from ever getting it together.

Will Buckley compares Beckham and Princess Diana, in the *Guardian*, 5 May 2004.

The bad news for Saddam Hussein is that he's just been sentenced to the death penalty. The good news for Saddam is that David Beckham is taking it.

Quoted by Matt Lawton in the *Daily Mail*, 5 July 2004.

Craig Bellamy

You've got both ends of the spectrum at Newcastle. On the one hand there's Alan Shearer, who is rightly regarded as an ambassador for the game, on the other hand you have Craig Bellamy.

Charlton Athletic goalkeeper Dean Kiely, quoted in the *Sunday Herald*, 2003.

Ronald and Frank de Boer

One's called Ronald,
One's called Frank,
One missed a penalty,
The other one's wank.

Chanted by Hibernian fans, after Frank de Boer had missed a penalty for Rangers.

Legends George Best

The extent to which George Best has fallen off the waggon was revealed today when his new liver asked for a free transfer to Paul Gascoigne.
Dead Ringers, BBC TV, 2004.

Not so much kiss-and-tell as pissed-and-tell.
Evening Standard, TV listing of the Channel 4 documentary *Alex Best: My Life with George*, spring 2004.

Peter Bonetti

With his ... spindly legs he looked like an accountant on a beach holiday who'd just wandered onto the pitch ... Gordon Banks with food poisoning would have still done better.

Nick Hancock, still fuming 25 years after Peter Bonetti's inept performance as Banks's replacement in the 1970 World Cup quarter-final against West Germany; in *Total Sport*, 1995.

Lee Bowyer

Down with the Ripper,
You're going down with the Ripper ...

Chanted by Chelsea fans after Bowyer was remanded on bail in connection with an alleged attack on an Asian student in 2000.

I don't think Lee Bowyer is racist at all; I think he would stamp on anyone's head.

Former England footballer Rodney Marsh on the same incident.

He's here, he's there, he wears no underwear,
Lee Bowyer, Lee Bowyer ...

Leeds fans' chant after Bowyer revealed in court that he sometimes goes out without underpants.

This is the man who was acquitted of an attack on a young lad in Leeds, but was found guilty of wearing black shoes with a metal buckle and no socks.

Football365.com, 'The Premiership Chav XI', 2004.

Tomas Brolin

I can't imagine him jumping for a ball. One of his eyelashes might come out.

George Graham, Leeds United manager, on releasing the Swede for whom he paid £4.5 million, in 1998. As the injury-prone Brolin piled on weight, the price was reckoned by some to be £1 per pound.

A chubby-faced hoover salesman.

The *Evening Standard*: 'Euro 2004: The Ultimate Guide'.

Legends — Sir Bobby Charlton

How much further down his head will Bobby Charlton have to part his hair before he faces the fact that he is bald?
Clive James, quoted in the *Guinness Book of Humorous Sports Quotes* (1996).

His reputation as a grizzlin' old miser was legendary.
Ron Atkinson, 1998.

Ooh, aah, French Wanka!

Eric Cantona gave interviews on art, philosophy and politics. A natural room-mate for David Batty, I thought, immediately.

Howard Wilkinson, *Managing to Succeed* (1992).

THE SH*T HITS THE FAN!

Headline in the *Daily Star* after Cantona's infamous kung-fu kick on an abusive Crystal Palace supporter in 1995. Brian Clough remarked of the incident: 'I would have cut off his testicles.'

Ooh, Aah, French Wanka!

Chant by West Ham fans following the king-fu incident, 'overheard' by comedienne Jo Brand. When Cantona was arrested over the incident, the *Sun* newspaper responded with the headline 'Ooh, Aah, Prisonaa!'

If a Frenchman goes on about seagulls, trawlers and sardines, he's called a philosopher. I'd just be called a short Scottish bum talking crap.

Gordon Strachan on Cantona's mystical musings on the attentions of the press, 1995. (The Frenchman's exact – and heavily accented – words were: 'When the seagulls follow a trawler, it is because they think sardines will be thrown into the sea.')

He's a footballer, a thug, and he's French.

Art critic Gavin Stamp explains why the National Portrait Gallery declined to hang a portrait of Cantona, 1997.

Paulo di Canio

On the striker's chance of a World Cup call-up:

Only if there's an outbreak of bubonic plague.

Italian manager Giovanni Trapattoni, 2002.

Stan Collymore

Brian wanted a Colly but all he got was a cabbage.

Tommy Docherty on Aston Villa manager Brian Little's disappointing acquisition, 1998.

I rang Alex Ferguson to see if he'd swap Collymore for Cole. He thought about it for a few seconds, then asked: 'How many bags?'

John Gregory, Little's successor as manager of Aston Villa, 1998.

Stan Collymore has joined Leicester City. Not to play – just to watch.

Joke circulating at the time of Collymore's revelation in March 2004 that he was a devotee of the sexual practice of 'dogging' (watching and engaging in outdoor sex).

Edgar Davids

He's a little dreadlock teapot!

Ian Wright, BBC TV, as the Dutch player leant casually against the goalpost during Holland v. Portugal, Euro 2004.

Augustin Delgado

Reporter: Gordon, Augustin Delgado?
Gordon Strachan: I've got more important things to think about. I've got a yoghurt to finish by today, the expiry date is today. That can be my priority, rather than Augustin Delgado.

Exchange quoted on the website 'The Motley Fool'; fool.co.uk.

Silly names Dickov and Titov

Whilst men wince at the implications of Paul Dickov's surname, it now seems that women watching Euro 2004 will have reason to do so as well. Spartak Moscow and Russia international Igor Titov should just be glad he doesn't play for Leeds, where we hear fans shout something that sounds like 'take that Titov' on a regular basis.

Anton Russell on laughfc.co.uk, 27 November 2003.

Mike Duxbury

I have seen things on *Star Trek: The Next Generation* that I find easier to believe than the fact that Mike Duxbury was once an England regular.

Nick Hancock, *Total Sport*, 1995.

Stefan Effenberg

I'm particularly unimpressed with the big midfielder Effenberg, who has been renamed in our house as Effenuseless.

Peter Corrigan on the former German player, in the *Independent on Sunday*, 1994 (see also Steven Gerrard, page 32).

Rio Ferdinand

He's out the England squad and we know why –
'Cos Rio got high,
Rio got high,
Rio got high,
la-la-la la-la-la.

Sung by rival fans (to the tune of Afroman's 'Cos I Got High') to remind Manchester United of the 8-month suspension of their star defender for failing to take a drugs test in 2003.

How outrageous that a so-called independent panel of experts wouldn't accept his cast-iron defence that the dog ate his appointment letter.

'Clogger' in the *Guardian*, 22 March 2004, on Rio Ferdinand's failure to get his ban for failing to turn up for a drugs test reduced.

Duncan Ferguson

A deranged Scotsman with strangulation, headlocks and wild gesticulation in his armoury.

'Clogger', in the *Guardian*, 22 March 2004.

Luis Figo

I can never forgive this. I don't want this to sound like a threat, but someone who does this to me will pay.

Barça president Joan Gaspart, after Figo left Barcelona for Real Madrid in 2001; quoted in the *Observer Sports Monthly*, 6 June 2004. When Figo returned to the Nou Camp in 2002, bottles, a knife and pig's head were thrown at him. One banner read: 'We hate you so much because we loved you so much.'

Robbie Fowler

So wrecked that he snorted salt for his tequila up his nose.

Anon. comment on Fowler's state when 'caught clubbing' in November 2003; quoted in the *Observer Sports Monthly*, 6 June 2004.

Paul Gascoigne

Daft as a brush.

Gazza's original nickname with his team-mates.

Comparing Gascoigne to Pelé is like comparing Rolf Harris to Rembrandt.

Rodney Marsh, former England footballer.

He has the brain-power of an iron filing.

Marcus Berkmann, *Punch*, 1992.

Silly names Argelico Fuks

ARGEL FUKS OFF TO BENFICA
Headline on the move to Spain of the Brazilian defender
Argelico Fuks, usually referred to by his nickname
of 'Argel'; quoted by Anton Russell on laughfc.co.uk,
6 November 2003.

On Gascoigne's signing for Lazio:

I'm pleased for him, but it's a bit like watching your
mother-in-law drive off a cliff in your new car.
Terry Venables, 1992.

He's fat, and he beats his wife ...
Sung by Chelsea fans (to the tune of the Pet Shop Boys' 'Go West').

I once said Gazza's IQ was less than his shirt
number and he asked me: 'What's an IQ?'
George Best, 1993.

Waddling around like a recently impregnated
hippopotamus ... Should football finally fail him,
at least there's a whole range of alternative careers
now on the horizon: Father Christmas ... barrage
balloon ... spacehopper.
Marcus Berkmann in the *Independent on Sunday*, 1993.

Steven Gerrard

Who is he?

Stefan Effenberg enquires as to the identity of the Liverpool midfielder before England's match with Germany, 2001. 'Effenuseless' (see page ??) found out soon enough, Gerrard scoring a crucial goal in England's 5–1 thrashing of their old enemy.

David Ginola

I love to pour my hot milky drink into your mug.

Graham Norton to the French footballing pin-up, describing the use to which he would like to put an Aston Villa mug adorned with Ginola's face. *So Graham Norton*, 2 March 2001.

Andy Goram

Two Andy Gorams, there's only two Andy Gorams.

Sung by Kilmarnock fans after the Rangers goalkeeper was diagnosed with mild schizophrenia.

Owen Hargreaves

He beats one, he beats two … he falls over.

Jonathan Northcroft in *The Sunday Times*, 27 June 2004.

John Hartson

Hartson's got more previous than Jack the Ripper.

Harry Redknapp.

The Hateleys — Like father, like son

Tony Hateley had it all. The only thing he lacked was ability.
Tommy Docherty on the much-travelled player of the 1960s.

A million quid for Mark Hateley? But he can't even trap a dead rat.
Stan Bowles.

What's it like living with a lunatic?
Anonymous phone caller to Hartson's girlfriend after the West Ham player's assault on team-mate Eyal Berkovic during training, 1998.

Emile Heskey

If Heskey plays for England so can I,
If Heskey plays for England so can I…
Sung by Birmingham fans as their team defeat Liverpool. 2004.

Glenn Hoddle

I hear Glenn Hoddle has found God. That must have been one hell of a pass.
Jasper Carrott.

Glenn Hoddle hasn't been the Hoddle we know.
Neither has Bryan Robson.

Ron Greenwood, English football manager, televised match commentary.

Glenn Hoddle … thought tackle was something
you put in your fishing bag.

Zit magazine, 1993.

Mark Hughes

He is playing better and better, even if he is going
grey and looking like a pigeon.

Gianluca Vialli, Chelsea player-manager, 1997.

Denis Irwin

A boring old shite.

Former Irish national team manager 'Big Jack' Charlton pays tribute to Irwin
at a testimonial dinner in Dublin, May 2000.

 **Norman Hunter**

**Norman Hunter does not tackle opponents so much as
break them down for resale as scrap.**
Julie Welch on the former Leeds player nicknamed 'Bites
Yer Legs' for the fierceness of his tackling.

Being Ruud — About goalkeepers

A goalkeeper is a goalkeeper because he can't play football.
Former Chelsea and Newcastle manager Ruud Gullit, 1997.

David James

David James, superstar,
Drops more bollocks than Grobbelaar.
Sung by Manchester United fans as their team beat Liverpool, 1997.

An accident waiting to happen.
Daniel Taylor, *The Guardian*, 19 February 2004, on the performance of 'Calamity James' in England's match against Portugal the night before.

England have no weak links. Well, except David James.
Switzerland's right-back Bernt Haas during Euro 2004, quoted in the *Guardian*, 17 June 2004.

Vinnie Jones

Vinnie Jones is to fine and fair football what Count Dracula was to blood transfusions.
Michael Herd in the *Evening Standard*, 1992.

Hard men? Well, there was that picture of Vinnie Jones holding Gazza's wotsits. In my day we called someone who did that a poof.

George Best, 1993.

Stone me! We've had cocaine, bribery and Arsenal scoring two goals at home. But just when you thought there were no surprises left in football, Vinnie Jones turns out to be an international player.

A gobsmacked Jimmy Greaves in the *Sun*, reacting to Vinnie Jones's being selected to play for Wales, 1994.

Ponderous as a carthorse and slow-witted … as a football donkey … it is hardly Jones's fault that such a clodhopper – sorry, former hod-carrier – has been able to wangle a prosperous living from the professional game.

Jeff Powell in the *Daily Mail*, 1996.

Roy Keane

He said to us, 'You all go with the flow.' I thought, 'Here we go again.' He'd been hammering me with the one-liners all week. I asked him 'What goes with the flow?' 'Dead fish,' he said. I thought: 'Wow! P-R-O-F-O-U-N-D! The Messiah has spoken.'

Jason McAteer on his Irish team-mate Roy Keane, May 2002; quoted in the *Guardian*, 1 July 2002.

I only ever hit Roy the once. He got up so I
couldn't have hit him very hard.

Brian Clough, Keane's manager when the Irishman was at Nottingham
Forest; quoted on forestfc.co.uk.

Kevin Keegan

The Julie Andrews of football.

Commentator Duncan McKenzie, 1981. But Julie Andrews never had a bubble
perm...

Is he always so funny? It's like watching the
Muppets.

German journalist in *Bild* magazine.

After George Best remarked that 'Kevin Keegan isn't fit to lace my boots':

Keegan isn't fit to lace Best's drinks.

John Roberts, quoted in the *Guinness Book of Humorous Sports Quotes*
(1996).

Jürgen Klinsmann

I've just seen Gary Lineker shake hands with
Jürgen Klinsmann – it's a wonder Klinsmann
hasn't fallen down.

Ron Atkinson, commentating on ITV during the 1990 World Cup semi-final.
Klinsmann had a certain reputation as a 'diver'.

Black Sheep Bitter: slips down easier than Jürgen Klinsmann.

Advertisement for the Yorkshire-brewed bitter, 1994.

Stan Lazarides

Because you're Australian and you always beat us at everything.

Referee David Elleray explains a booking for Birmingham City's Stan Lazarides, Quotes of the Year, www.telegraph.co.uk, 30 December 2003.

Anagrams — The all-time top ten

David Ginola = O! A diving lad
A living gonad
Vagina dildo

Martin Keown = I'm not wanker

Diego Maradona = Oh dear, I'm a gonad

Paul Merson = Lump on arse

Fabrizio Ravanelli = Evil Brazilian Afro

Alan Shearer = Her anal arse

Teddy Sheringham = He'd shag dirty men

Gareth Southgate = Treat to huge shag

Graeme Le Saux

Nobody cares if Le Saux is gay or not. It is the fact that he openly admits to reading the *Guardian* that makes him the most reviled man in football.

Piers Morgan, editor of the *Mirror*, 1999.

Gary Lineker

The Queen Mother of football.

Arthur Smith and Chris England, *An Evening With Gary Lineker* (1990).

Claus Lundekvam

When he was carried off at Leicester someone asked me if he was unconscious, but I didn't have a clue – that's what he's always like.

Southampton manager Gordon Strachan, quoted in the *Sunday Herald*, 2003.

Rodney Marsh

Playing with Rodney Marsh is like playing alongside Barbra Streisand.

Mike Summerbee, 1973, quoted in the *Guinness Book of Humorous Sports Quotes* (1996).

Paul Merson

Paul has had his problems but we've got people here who like wearing dresses and having their bottoms spanked, so he should fit in well.

John Gregory of Aston Villa, on becoming Merson's manager in 1998. The 'people' referred to, Dwight Yorke and Mark Bosnich, had been the subject of a tabloid exposé.

Savo Milosevic

The most one-footed player since Long John Silver.

Letter to the Birmingham *Evening Mail*, 1997.

Villa fans saw him aim a spit at them – but, knowing him, he would probably have missed.

Another tribute to 'Misalotevic', from the Aston Villa fanzine following the club's 5–0 defeat against Blackburn, 1998.

Jan Molby

Jan Molby looked corpulent enough to be playing darts for Denmark.

Brian Glanville in *The Sunday Times*, 1985.

Maradona

One hideous chapter after another ...

If there is an effective way of killing off the threat of Diego Maradona by marking him, it probably involves putting a white cross over his heart and tethering him to a stake in front of a firing squad.

Hugh McIlvanney in the *Observer*, 1986.

Diego Armando Maradona ... is from the backside of Buenos Aires.

An unintended insult from US journalist Rick Telander on SI.com, 14 May 1990.

The little tear jerk ...

Cris Freddi on Maradona's crying after Argentina's defeat in the 1990 World Cup final, in the *Guinness Book of Sporting Blunders* (1994).

His contorted features made him look like a lunatic, flying on a cocktail of every drug known to man.

The *Guardian* on Maradona's appearance during the 1994 World Cup (after which he was banned for drug abuse).

MARAGONER!

Headline in the *New York Daily News* following Maradona's positive drugs test at the 1994 World Cup.

One hideous chapter after another.
The *Guardian* sums up Maradona's career, April 2004.

By comparison with Diego Armando Maradona, the descent of a George Best or a Paul Gascoigne seems almost decorous, just as his history of dalliances makes David Beckham's alleged extracurricular activities look like the adventures of a boy scout.
The *Guardian*, April 2004.

He went to parties dressed as Osama Bin Laden holding a toy machine-gun and loved night-time golf. The bloated former world cup winner would play shots by torchlight using phosphorescent balls.
Martin Chilton in the *Evening Standard*, 4 May 2004, describing Maradona's lifestyle at the La Pradera health farm in Havana.

'll probably call it the Matthews funeral.
ie Guardian, 1991, reporting on the funeral of Stan
Mortensen. Despite Mortensen's hat-trick for Blackpool,
the 1953 FA Cup Final has been known ever since as 'The
Matthews Final' for Matthews's role in setting up the goals.

Gary Neville

The balletic poise of a three-legged hippo.
'Clogger' of the *Guardian* on the Manchester United and England defender,
16 February 2004.

Paul Scholes with four players in front of him – five if you count Gary Neville.
Commentator Darragh Moloney.

He does not look much like a male model, and his
personal life, one suspects, has not presented him
with too many problems of the babe-magnet
variety. The Sunday red tops struggle to find many
juicy revelations. Somehow, some bimbo saying: 'I
looked down at my breasts and there was Gary
Neville' does not have a ring of authenticity.
John Rawling in the *Guardian*, 26 April 2004.

Carlton Palmer

Carlton Palmer can trap the ball further than I can kick it.

Ron Atkinson.

Carlton Palmer is the worst finisher since Devon Loch.

Ron Atkinson, 1991. Devon Loch, the Queen Mother's horse, notoriously fell when about to win the Grand National in 1956.

He covers every blade of grass – but that's just because his first touch is crap.

Dave Jones, Southampton manager, 1997.

Robert Pires

Count on Robert Pires to keep his D'Artagnan beard nicely trimmed so he looks *formidable* as he crumples to the turf just inside the box under a non-existent challenge.

The *Guardian*, 'Euro 2004:The Definitive Guide', 7 June 2004.

David Platt

… an agent's dream: good enough to earn a decent move, but never good enough for a club to keep.

David Hills on the former England midfielder, in the *Observer Sports Monthly*, 6 June 2004.

Mick Quinn

He's fat, he's round,
He's worth a million pound.

Chanted by Portsmouth fans.

Who ate all the pies?
Who ate all the pies?
You fat bastard,
You fat bastard,
You ate all the pies!

Chanted by rival Aston Villa fans at the man nicknamed 'Sumo' during his spell at Coventry City. Quinn later used the taunt as the title of his autobiography (2003).

Jamie Redknapp

He has as much bite and penetration as you would expect from a Spurs midfielder.

The Times, June 2004, on Redknapp as a football pundit.

Laurent Robert

Robert said I was picking the wrong team. At the time I was – because he was in it.

Newcastle manager Sir Bobby Robson on Lauren Robert; 'Quotes of the Week', bbc.co.uk, November 2003.

Legends | Alf Ramsey

Ramsey, tha's as much use as a chocolate teapot.
Shouted by a fan to Ramsey when England's future
World-Cup winning manager was a right-back with
Southampton in the 1940s. Quoted in David Pickering
Cassell's Soccer Companion (1994).

Jason Roberts

You are talking about a man who spelt his name
wrong on his transfer request.
West Bromwich Albion manager Gary Megson on his former player's move to
Wigan Athletic; quoted on the Sky Sports Planet Football website.

Ronaldo

The Brazilian chipmunk.
Peter FitzSimons on smh.com.au., 6 July 2002.

He arrived like a king. He leaves like a thief.
Italy's *Corriere dello Sport* on Ronaldo's desertion of Inter Milan for Real
Madrid, quoted in the *Observer Sports Monthly*, 6 June 2004. Inter had paid
Ronaldo's reputed £75,000 per week wages and funded treatment and
counselling during Ronaldo's lengthy injury lay-off.

Rooooney Forget Gazza, here's Wazza

King of the boy Chavs ... Picture him screaming 'You
fucking cunt!' at a referee with a spotty face (Rooney,
not the referee) or chewing gum on the *BBC Sports
Personality of the Year* awards with a fat, skew-whiff tie.
Not just the future of football, but the future of Chavvery.
Football365.com, 'The Premiership Chav XI', 2004.

He's fat, he's Scouse, He'll rob your fucking house ...
Pub chant popular during Euro 2004.

Rooney seems to have modelled his style of play on the baby elephant that ran amok in the *Blue Peter* studio.

Simon Barnes, 'Baby elephant brings the house down', in *The Times*, 18 June 2004; after Rooney scored twice in England v. Switzerland, Euro 2004.

The new Pelé? Don't make us retch.

'Are comparisons between Rooney and Pelé Over the Top?', in the *Guardian*, 23 June 2004.

Forget Gazza, here's Wazza.

Daniel Taylor in the *Guardian*, 24 June 2004, reporting that England's players have adapted the Gazza moniker for their new star.

Roy of the Rovers with the physique of Desperate Dan.

Andrew Anthony in the *Guardian*, 24 June 2004.

Michael Owen used to be the baby-faced assassin, Rooney is more like the assassin-faced baby.

The *Guardian*, during Euro 2004.

Unlike the fancy-pants multilinguals at Arsenal and Chelsea he looks more like a fan than the fans do … he has the potato face and the awful hair and the clamorous family that they have.

Novelist Justin Cartwright in the *Evening Standard*, 25 June 2004.

Better than Platini. No, Maradona. No, Pelé!!! Okay, as injury-prone as Darren Anderton.

Ian Chadband in the *Evening Standard*, 2 July 2004.

Paul Scholes

Paul Scholes can't score goals any more and looks like a gonk with a French crop.

Tim Lott in the *Evening Standard*, 10 June 2004.

To me Paul Scholes has always just been a ginger Nick Barmby.

Harry Pearson in the *Guardian*, 3 July 2004.

David Seaman

Q: Why do Spanish men make great lovers?
A: Because they can lob Seaman from 40 yards.

Joke current in 1995, when Seaman's goalkeeping gaffe in the final of the European Cup Winner's Cup let in a speculative lob from the half-way line by Real Zaragoza's Nayim (a former Tottenham player).

That Seaman is a handsome young man but he spends too much time looking in his mirror, rather than at the ball. You can't keep goal with hair like that.

Brian Clough on Seaman's ponytail; quoted on forestfc.co.uk.

How clean sheets can be associated with a man who has a porn star's moustache and pony-tail, as well as having the name David Seaman, we'll never know – at least at [Manchester] City he's got rid of the clean sheet link.

Anton Russell on laughfc.co.uk, 11 December 2003.

[He] cost his country what ever fading chance it had of a World Cup, reacting to danger with the speed and agility of Andy Fordham after 27 pints and a lamb bhuna.

Matthew Norman in the *Evening Standard*, 19 January 2004, referring to Seaman's failure to save Ronaldinho's lob in England's 2002 World Cup quarter-final with Brazil.

And which of them – the heroic Martin Johnson or that preening ponytailed ponce David Seaman – won about 75% of the media coverage devoted to their retirements over the weekend?

Matthew Norman on the retirements of England's rugby world-cup winning England captain Johnson and former England goalkeeper Seaman.

If David Seaman's dad had worn a condom, we'd still be in the World Cup.

Nick Hancock, BBC TV *They Think It's All Over*, 6 February 2004.

Comic names have rarely coincided with on-field success. Harry Daft won five England caps, but Segar Bastard was shunned after one. Brazil's Rafael Scheidt was a self-fulfilling prophesy at Celtic. Daniel Killer, the Argentinian defender of the 1970s, was kind to children and animals. And the Australian goalkeeper Norman Conquest is merely a footnote in history.

'Clogger' in the *Guardian*, 24 February 2004.

Alan Shearer

A man so dull he once made the papers for having a one-in-a-bed romp.

Nick Hancock, *They Think It's All Over*, BBC TV 1997.

… Shearer is boring – we call him Mary Poppins.

Newcastle United director Freddie Shepherd, secretly taped by the *News of the World*, 1998. Shearer replied that he'd been called worse: 'Tim Flowers once called me football's answer to Nigel Mansell.'

… Shearer bleats like a neurotic nun goosed by a passing monsignor.

Matthew Norman in the *Evening Standard*, 1 March 2004. On Shearer's disappointment at being rested by Sir Bobby Robson for a UEFA cup tie, February 2004.

Peter Shilton

Peter Shilton, Peter Shilton,
Does your missus know you're here?

Sung by Chelsea fans (to the tune of *Cwm Rhondda*) after the then
Nottingham Forest keeper was disturbed *in flagrante* in a country lane with a
woman called Tina, 1980. When Tina's husband arrived, Shilton drove away in
haste, crashing into a lamp-post.

Ole Gunnar Solksjaer

You are my Solskjaer, my Ole Solskjaer,
You make me happy when skies are grey,
And Alan Shearer was fucking dearer,
So please don't take my Solskjaer away.

Sung by Manchester United fans in honour of their baby-faced Norwegian
striker, to the tune of 'You Are My Sunshine.'

Graeme Souness

They serve a drink in Glasgow called a Souness –
one half and you're off.

Tommy Docherty.

Gareth Southgate

Why didn't you just belt it, son?

Southgate's mother to her son after his notorious miss in the penalty
shoot-out with Germany in the Euro 1996 semi-final.

Q: What's the quickest way out of Wembley
   Stadium?
A: The Southgate.

Just when we thought his compatriots had no sense of humour, a German
listener phones Heart FM in 1998 with this commemoration of Southgate's
penalty miss.

Hard men Nobby Stiles

**Nobby Stiles a dirty player? No, he's never hurt anyone.
Mind you, he's frightened a few.**

Sir Matt Busby on the man nicknamed variously the
'Toothless Tiger' and (for his ruthless tackling against
Argentina in the 1966 World Cup) 'El Bandito'.

Pierre van Hooijdonk

If someone offered me an olive branch I'd stick it up his arse.

Dave Bassett, Nottingham Forest manager, 1997, after the Dutchman went on strike, complaining that the team was sub-standard and going abroad to sulk.

Ruud van Nistelrooy

What a player. Even when he farts he seems to score.

Alessandro del Piero of Juventus on Ruud van Nistelrooy, quoted on bbc.co.uk, 24 May 2003.

Patrick Vieira

Vieira, oo-ooh!
Vieira, oo-ooh!
He comes from Senegal,
His dad's a cannibal.

Sung by opposing fans to the tune of Dean Martin's 'Volare'.

Christian Vieri

Once the most rambunctious target-man in Europe, the Internazionale forward now heads the ball with his eyes shut and an expression on his face that calls to mind a spaniel about to be struck with a rolled-up newspaper.

Harry Pearson in the *Guardian*, 3 July 2004.

These days [Viera] is so covered in ink he looks as if a junior executive has used him as a doodle pad …

Harry Pearson on Vieri's tattoos, in the *Guardian*, 3 July 2004.

Chris Waddle

The mullet king.

Cris Freddi in *Footballers' Haircuts* (2003).

Dennis Wise

He would start a fight in an empty house.

Alex Ferguson, quoted on BBC Radio 4's Today programme, 5 April 2004.

We had probably our best-ever Player of the Year Dance last week. You elected Dennis Wise as Player of the Year. Dennis accepted his award mimicking Vialli, whereupon Zola shouted 'Speak English'. Dennis switched to his normal Cockney voice only for Zola to shout 'You're still not speaking English.'

Chelsea Chairman Ken Bates, programme notes, November 1998.

Ninety-five per cent of my language problems are the fault of that stupid little midget.

Gianfranco Zola remembers his former Chelsea team-mate Dennis Wise; quoted on bbc.co.uk, 2004.

Nicknames — The all-time top ten

Darren Anderton = Sicknote (for his frequent injuries)

Roberto Baggio = the Divine Ponytail (for his coiffure at the 1990 World Cup)

John Barnes = Tarmac (from Barnes's original nickname 'the black Heighway', Steve Heighway being a Liverpool winger of the 1970s)

Dennis Bergkamp = the Non-Flying Dutchman (from his fear of flying, punning on the opera by Wagner)

Duncan Ferguson = Duncan Disorderly (from Ferguson's conviction during his time in Scotland)

Jesper Gronkjaer = Dracula (for the Dane's supposed 'fear of crosses')

David James = Calamity James (for his goalkeeping errors, punning on Calamity Jane, nickname of the American frontierwoman Martha Jane Burke)

Savo Milosevic = Misalotevic (for the Serb's inability to score)

Mick Quinn = Sumo (for his generous girth)

Wayne Rooney = Shrek or the Croxteth Cruncher (for his being no oil-painting, and for his vigorous style of play)

Who the f***?

Tom Thumb, Snow White, and Quasimodo are sitting talking.

Tom Thumb says, 'How do I know I'm the world's smallest man? Maybe I'm NOT the world's smallest man.' He becomes very depressed.

Then Snow White says, 'How do I know I'm the most beautiful woman in the world? Perhaps there is someone more beautiful than me!' And she too becomes very depressed.

Quasimodo then says, 'How do I know I'm the world's ugliest man? Maybe there is someone even uglier than me!' And he, too, sinks into depression.

A week later Tom Thumb, Snow White, and Quasimodo are all tragically killed in a horrific car crash. While waiting at the Pearly Gates, each of them is invited to a private meeting with God, who says that he will answer one question for each of them.

After Tom Thumb's meeting, he comes out smiling and says, 'It's all right, I am indeed the world's smallest man!'

Snow White also emerges from her meeting wreathed in smiles. 'It's OK,' she says. 'I am the fairest of them all!'

Quasimodo, however, comes out of his meeting scratching his head. He looks at the others and asks,

'Who the fuck is Martin Keown?'

Internet joke.

Frank Worthington

… the breakdown of his move to Liverpool in 1972 is one of the game's enduring urban legends. Having all but signed, the deal fell through because he failed a medical. The rumour was that he had a dose of the clap. In fact he had high blood pressure … brought on by excessive sexual activity.

In the *Observer Sport Monthly*, 'The 10 worst examples of footballers behaving badly', 4 November, 2001. Worthington's idiosyncratic biography was entitled *One Hump or Two?* When asked in 1993 how many clubs he had played for, Worthington responded: 'I had 11 clubs – 12 if you count Stringfellows.'

Dwight Yorke

The footballer the fans call the King of Pornography.

Jordan in *Being Jordan: My Autobiography* (2004).

Dwight was very selfish in bed … Dwight had the extra inches but the chemistry between us wasn't that strong.

Jordan again.

Zinedine Zidane

Zinedine Zidane could be a champion sumo wrestler. He can run like a crab or a gazelle.

A strangely insulting compliment from Howard Wilkinson.

Zinedine Zidane was fantastic for two minutes.
Shame about the other 358.

Ian Chadband on Zidane's performance at Euro 2004; in the *Evening
Standard*, 2 July 2004.

Gianfranco Zola

He's always got an Italian–English phrasebook
with him. Mind you, that's for him to stand on.

Graeme Le Saux of Chelsea, on the diminutive Italian star, 1998.

■ FOOTBALL CLUBS
(mainly) as others see them

A bad football team is like an old bra – no cups and little support.

Anon.

Arsenal

Are you Arsenal?
Are you Arsenal?
Are you Arsenal in disguise?

Taunt sung to any team considered to be playing boringly.

It is the right of every Englishman at a football match to fall asleep if he wants, particularly if he's watching Arsenal.

Judge Michael Taylor, overturning the conviction for drunkenness of Adrian Carr, a Middlesbrough fan who dozed off while his team were losing 4–0 to Arsenal.

Who let the frogs out?
Who? Who? Who? Who?

A punning reference to Arsenal's French-dominated team under Arsène Wenger; sung to the tune of the Baha Men's 'Who Let the Dogs Out?'.

Who put the ball in the Arsenal net?
Half of fucking Europe!
Reflecting Arsenal's shaky performances in European competition in the 2000s.

Aston Villa

I just wanted to give my players some technical advice. I told them the game had started.
Manager Ron Atkinson explains why he stood on the touchline, 1990s.

Someone asked me ... if I missed the Villa. I said, 'No, I live in one.'
David Platt, after he moved from Aston Villa to the Italian club Bari, 1991.

Birmingham City

Birmingham City,
Birmingham City,
100 years and won fuck all,
Birmingham City.
Especially popular with rival Aston Villa fans.

You lose some, you draw some.
Jasper Carrott on being a Birmingham City fan, 1978.

Blackburn Rovers

Blackburn is so poor and ugly. I couldn't bear to live there one more day … You can't do that to your family.

Dutch international Richard Witschge explains why he chose not to extend his loan spell at Ewood Park, 1996.

They've snubbed me? Do me a favour. Let's face it, would I want to go there?

Paul Ince, responding to reports that he had been rejected by Blackburn Rovers as being 'past his peak', 1997.

Bradford City

Small town in Asia,
You're just a small town in Asia …

Sung by rival fans to the tune of Los Tres Paraguayos' 1970s hit 'Guantanamera'.

Basement blues

Down in a minute,
We're going down in a minute …

Sung to the tune of 'Guantanamera' again by Bradford City fans as their team were losing 2–1 to Everton with a minute to go of the 2001 Premiership season.

Bristol Rovers

I remember with Villa when we played Bristol
Rovers at Twerton Park. I kept saying to the boys:
'You're going to the arsehole of the world. Think
of the worst you can and it's worse than that.'
Ron Atkinson.

Burnley

Always look on the Turf Moor for shite,
Da-da, da-da-da-da-da-da.
Sung, with many variations, to the tune of 'Always Look on the Bright Side of
Life'.

Carlisle United

I could have signed for Newcastle when I was 17,
but I decided I would be better off at Carlisle. I'd
had a drink that night.
Peter Beardsley looks back, 1994.

Celtic

See The Auld Firm, pages 80–81.

Chelsea

Shit team in Fulham,
You're just a shit team in Fulham…

Sung by Arsenal fans, again to the tune of 'Guantanamera'.

When I first heard about Viagra I thought it was a new player Chelsea had just signed.

Sports minister and Chelsea fan Tony Banks, referring in 1998 to the preponderance of foreign players in the Chelsea side.

Never let a Chelsea player take your dog for a walk – because they cannot hang on to a lead.

Andrew Dillon in the *Sun*, 2 January 2002; Chelsea had led Southampton 2–0 before going down 4–2.

Chester City

Your mother is your sister,
Your father is your brother,
You like to shag each other –
The Chester Family.

Taunting Chester City FC (to the theme tune of *The Addams Family*).

You're Welsh and you know you are,
You're Welsh and you know you are…

Another taunt for Chester City (to the tune of 'Go West'); also sung to taunt Shrewsbury Town and Hereford United.

Doncaster Rovers

You wouldn't take the kids along for fear they might catch something.

Mark Weaver, acting manager, on the club's ground facilities, 1998.

Everton

See Kop Out, page 70.

Galatasaray

You're shish, and you know you are,
You're shish, and you know you are ...

Sung by Chelsea fans: a punning variation, for the Turkish context, of 'You're shit ...', again to the tune of 'Go West'.

Leeds United

The bloke next to me is reading *American Psycho*. It may well be the only book Leeds fans have ever read.

John Aizlewood, *Playing At Home* (1999).

All the qualities of a dog except loyalty.

David Mellor on Leeds United players during their horror season 2003–04, in the *Evening Standard* 23 January 2004. Warming to his theme, Mellor went on: 'Leeds have 18 players on more than £1 million a year, and most are useless.'

3:0   Leeds and Manchester DisUnited

On your Yorkshire farms,
You pester the lambs when you hide in the grass,
You'd rather shag sheep than a fit normal lass,
On your Yorkshire farms ...

Sung by Manchester United fans (to the tune of the
Spinners' 'In My Liverpool Home').

He's red, he's white,
He knew Leeds were shite,
Cantona, Cantona ...

Leeds are our feeder club,
Leeds are our feeder club ...

Both of the above (the second to the tune of 'Go West')
were popular with Manchester United fans after Eric
Cantona's move from Leeds to Manchester United in
November 1992.

Reports that Dido is stepping out with Alan Smith
must be making the tabloids drool. It's quite apt,
really, her last big hit was 'White Flag'. His team
have been waving one all season.

'Clogger' in the *Guardian*, April 2004, on the then Leeds striker before he left
relegated Leeds for Manchester United.

Bust in a fortnight,
You're going bust in a fortnight …

Sung by almost everybody ('Guantanamera', yet again), until the club's small shareholders made the ultimate sacrifice, 2004.

eBay gum, it's Leeds

Headline in the *Evening Standard* after an advert for the Elland Road ground was placed on the the auction web site eBay.

Leicester City

Score in La Manga,
You couldn't score in La Manga …

Sung by Birmingham City fans ('Guantanamera' again) in Leicester's first match after three of their players were charged with sexual assault during a 'team bonding' trip to the Spanish resort of La Manga, March 2004.

Originally there was only one German woman in the room with the Leicester players, but as usual they let in two more in the last minute.

Internet joke about the La Manga episode.

Walker's are bringing out a new crisp flavour: Assault 'n' Finger.

Another internet joke, at the expense of Leicester's sponsor.

Violent, aggressive, drunken, misogynistic, socially inept morons who shouldn't be out on their own, let alone be representing a Premiership club.

Carole Malone in the *Sunday Mirror* on the players involved in the La Manga episode. In May 2004 DNA evidence cleared the players of all charges.

Liverpool

In your Liverpool slums,
In your Liverpool slums,
Your mum's on the game and your dad's in the
    nick,
You can't get a job 'cause you're so fucking thick,
In your Liverpool slums.

In your Liverpool slums,
You look in the dustbin for something to eat,
You find a dead dog and you think it's a treat,
There's piss on the pavements and shit in the
    street,
In your Liverpool slums.

Sung to the tune of the Spinners' 'In My Liverpool Home' (also applied, with variants, to other clubs; see also Leeds and Manchester DisUnited, page 67).

Liverpool are my nap selection – I prefer to sleep when they're on the box.

Former QPR star and keen gambler Stan Bowles gives his verdict on Liverpool's style of play; quoted on bbc.co.uk, 'Quotes of the Week', September 2003.

Fear and loathing on Merseyside

BLUE ON RED:

Oh we hate Bill Shankly,
And we hate St John,
But most of all we hate Big Ron,
And we'll hang the Kopites one by one,
On the banks of the Royal Blue Mersey.
Sung to the tune of 'The Halls of Montezuma'.

You can stick your Michael Owen up your arse,
You can stick your Michael Owen up your arse …
And so on ad infinitum, to the tune of 'She'll be Coming
Round the Mountain'.

RED ON BLUE:

If Everton were playing down at the bottom of my
garden, I'd draw the curtains.
Bill Shankly.

The city has two great teams –
Liverpool and Liverpool reserves.
Bill Shankly.

I've achieved nothing, I've won nothing, and that's why I am here.

Former Leeds player Harry Kewell explains why he has signed for Liverpool; quoted in the *Sunday Herald*, 2003.

Bore on, bore on, no hope in your hearts …

The *Guardian*, 22 March 2004.

Manchester City

Apparently Man City are hoping to exploit fully the Bosman ruling in order to play 11 Germans. That way they can go down with all Hans.

Martin Thorpe in the *Guardian*, 1996, referring to the 'Bosman ruling', which eased restrictions on the signing of foreign players.

We're shit, and we're sick of it,
We're shit …

Sung by their own fans (to the tune of 'Go West') during yet another light blue low ebb, 1997.

May I wish Joe Royle well in a task equivalent to nailing jelly to a ceiling?

Welcoming another new manager to Maine Road; letter to the *Manchester Evening News*, 1998.

It's a rat-infested place.

A parting shot from another ex-Manchester City manager, Frank Clark, 1998.

I've had enough. As soon as I get home I'm gonna buy that club. I'm gonna walk in and say, 'You … fuck off; you … fuck off; you … fuck off; you … make me a cup of tea.'

Enraged Manchester City fan Noel Gallagher, quoted in the *Daily Telegraph*, 28 December 1998.

Ouch! Light blue for laughing-stock

There are three types of Oxo cubes: Light brown for chicken stock, dark brown for beef stock – and light blue for laughing-stock.

Tommy Docherty, former Manchester United manager, 1988. Quoted in David Pickering *Cassell's Soccer Companion* (1994).

Two–nil up and fucked it up,
City, City,
Two–nil up and fucked it up,
City is our name …

Sung (to the tune of 'Camptown Races') by Manchester United fans (and others, with different numbers), mocking the club's shaky defensive record under Kevin Keegan in the 2000s.

Manchester United

Q: Can you name three football clubs with a rude
    word in their name?
A: Arsenal, Scunthorpe, and fucking Manchester
    United.

A *very* old joke.

In your Manchester scrubs,
You speak with accents that no-one can stand,
You're ugly fat bastards with shit on yer hands,
In your Manchester scrubs.

Sung by Liverpool supporters (to the tune of 'In My Liverpool Home').

Next to Barça, Manchester United look like
Rochdale. Manchester United do not have a
weekly satirical TV programme devoted to them,
and nor do they run an art competition so
prestigious that Salvador Dali once submitted an
entry, nor boast the Pope as season ticket holder
no. 108,000.

Simon Kuper, *Football against the Enemy* (1994).

Q: What do you think of Manchester United?
A: They're cheating, whingeing scumbags.

Comedian Rory McGrath answering a questionnaire in *Total Sport* magazine,
1997.

PC? Virus problem at Old Trafford

The Alex Ferguson virus: your PC develops a continuous whining noise.

The Roy Keane virus: throws you out of Windows.

The Massimo Taibi virus: you can't save anything.
Internet jokes, *c*.2001.

Manchester United Ruined My Life.
Book title, Colin Shindler (1998).

Manchester United in Brazil? I hope they all get bloody diarrhoea.
Brian Clough on Alex Ferguson's decision to withdraw from the FA Cup in favour of the World Club Championship, January 2000.

Mansfield Town

To say I'm bitterly disappointed is an understatement. They've got the footballing brains collectively of a rocking-horse.
Mansfield manager Keith Curle after his side's 1–1 draw with Orient; 'Quotes of the Week', bbc.co.uk, August 2003.

Middlesbrough

Middlesbrough signing [Fabrizio] Ravanelli is like someone buying a Ferrari without having a garage.

Giancarlo Galavotti, Italian sports journalist, 1996.

Millwall

You are the Millwall,
The only Millwall,
Nobody likes you,
'Cos you're shit.

Sung to the tune of Jimmy Davis and Charles Mitchell's 'You Are My Sunshine', in mockery of the Millwall chant, 'Nobody likes us and we don't care, 'cos we are the Millwall'.

Basement blues

Now we all know where you're going,
So fuck off, enjoy the ride:
Morecambe and Southport and Dover,
Stalybridge, Welling and Hyde.

Sung (with variations) to any club about to be relegated from the league to the Nationwide Conference; first recorded at Hereford v. Brighton, May 1997 (when Brighton avoided the drop).

Personally, I like a hostile environment. Maybe it's because I played at Millwall.

Kasey Keller, US goalkeeper, on the prospect of facing Iran, 1998.

The prospect of Millwall qualifying for the UEFA Cup has brought about a review of government defence spending.

Clive Tyldesley in the *Daily Telegraph*, 19 March 2004, as the club progressed to the FA Cup semi-finals.

Nottingham Forest

They could put ten dustbins out there and do the job they do.

Terry McDermott, 1980.

All Nottingham has is Robin Hood, and he's dead.

Dutchman Bryan Roy, on leaving the club, 1997.

Oldham Athletic

Oldham Athletic? That's a contradiction in terms.

Coronation Street, ITV; quoted in the *Guinness Book of Humorous Sports Quotes* (1996).

Partick Thistle

For years I thought the club's name was Partick Thistle Nil.

Billy Connolly joke, *c.*1980, quoted in David Pickering, *Cassell's Soccer Companion* (1994).

As a small boy I was torn between two ambitions: to be a footballer or to run away and join a circus. At Partick Thistle I got to do both.

Alan Hansen, a former Thistle player, 1997.

Portsmouth

Fratton Park is falling down,
Falling down, falling down,
Fratton Park is falling down,
Poor old Pompey…

If I had the wings of a sparrow,
If I had the arse of a crow,
I'd fly over Fratton tomorrow,
And shit on the bastards below, below,
Shit on the bastards below …

Two chants popular with fans of Portsmouth's bitter rivals, Southampton.

Shit ground no fans,
Shit ground no fans ...
Originally sung by Southampton fans when playing
Portsmouth at Fratton Park; now universal.

Queen of the South

See Watford, page 82.

Rangers

See The Auld Firm, page 80–81.

Real Madrid

The most educated person at Real Madrid is the
woman who cleans the lavatories.

Barcelona vice-president Joan Gaspart on the club's officials, 1997.

Southampton

I have never seen so much acne on a football
pitch.

Gordon Strachan on a Southampton reserve team game, quoted on
laughfc.co.uk.

Stoke City

You're Stoke,
You're a fucking joke …

Sung to the tune of 'Go West'.

Sunderland

Where the hell did Sunderland get the
unmitigated gall to call their new ground
'The Stadium Of Light'?

Danny Kelly, 'Football's Great Imponderables', on Football365.com.

Tottenham Hotspur

White Hart Lane is a great place. The only thing
wrong is the seats face the pitch.

Comedian Les Dawson, 1991.

Wimbledon with fans.

Former Spurs star Jimmy Greaves's verdict in 1999.

If I have the chance to go to England, I will aim
on a level below Arsenal. I like Tottenham very
much.

Antoine Sibierski, midfielder with the French club Lens, quoted in the *Sunday Herald*, 2003.

The Auld Firm

Fear and loathing in Glesca

One team in Glasgow,
There's only one team in Glasgow ...
Sung by fans of Partick Thistle.

You are a weegie,
A smelly weegie,
You're only happy on giro day,
Your mum's a stealer,
Your dad's a dealer,
Please don't take my hubcaps away.
Sung by Dundee fans to both sides of the Auld Firm, to the
tune of 'You Are My Sunshine'. A 'weegie' is a Glaswegian.

Whenever I'm in time of trouble,
Mother Mary comes to me,
Singing Celtic 1, Caley 3.
Celtic 1, Caley 3,
Celtic 1, Caley 3,
Singing Celtic 1, Caley 3.
Sung by Rangers fans in celebration of Celtic's humiliation
(to the tune of Simon and Garfunkel's 'Bridge Over
Troubled Water').

SUPER CALEY GO BALLISTIC, CELTIC ARE ATROCIOUS

Headline in the Scottish edition of the *Sun* following lowly Inverness Caledonian Thistle's giantkilling 3–1 Scottish FA Cup victory over Celtic, February 2000.

Bless Them All, Bless Them All, Bless Them All!
The Pope and St Vincent de Paul!
Fuck your King Billy 'cos he's down in hell,
And fuck your John Knox, 'cos he's down there as well.

Only in Glasgow can a football chant make reference to the Roman Catholic founder (in 1634) of the Order of the Sisters of Charity and the Protestant author (in 1558) of *The first blast of the trumpet against the monstrous regiment of women*; sung by Celtic fans to taunt Rangers.

You'll be watching *The Bill* when we're in Seville…

Celtic fans to Rangers fans, reminding them that Celtic are in the 2003 UEFA Cup Final.

We were watching *The Bill* – what was the score in Seville?

The response of Rangers fans after Celtic's 3–2 UEFA Cup Final defeat by Porto, May 2003.

An anxious woman goes to her doctor. 'Doctor,' she asks nervously, 'can you get pregnant from anal intercourse?' 'Certainly,' replies the doctor. 'Where do you think Auld Firm fans come from?'

Internet joke.

Kasey Keller ... was spotted at the cinema enjoying the movie *Along Came Polly* ... According to critics the film starts promisingly and then deteriorates in the second half – nothing new for a Spurs player, then.

'The Talk in Football', *Evening Standard*, 11 March 2004.

Watford

Elton John decided he wanted to rename Watford, he wanted to call it Queen of the South.

Tommy Docherty, quoted in the *Guinness Book of Humorous Sports Quotes* (1996).

West Bromwich Albion

Oh I do like to be beside the seaside,
Oh I do like to be beside the sea,
Oh I do like to stroll along the prom, prom, prom,
Where the brass bands play 'Fuck off West Brom'.

Since transferred to other clubs, but this version rhymes the best.

Always shit in a Tesco carrier bag,
Di-dum, di-dum, di-dum, di-dum, di-dum ...

Sung to the tune of *Always Look on the Bright Side of Life* and a favourite among Wolves fans. The WBA strip bears blue stripes not dissimilar to those on a Tesco carrier bag, and the club's nickname is 'The Baggies'.

Baa — What's it like to shag a sheep?

Give us a B (B!)
Give us an A (A!)
Give us an A (A!)
What's that spell?
Baaaaaaaaaa!
Taunting fans of any rural or Welsh club.

What's it like, what's it like,
What's it like to shag a sheep?
Sung to the tune of *Cwm Rhondda*.

Failed in Wales,
Failed in Wales,
Cardiff, Swansea and Wrexham.
Cardiff, Swansea and Wrexham.
Anti-Welsh taunt based on the *Not The Nine O'Clock News* spoof of the promotional advert 'Made in Wales', again sung to the tune of *Cwm Rhondda*.

West Ham United

Chim chimeney, chim chimeney,
Chim chim cheroo,
We hate those bastards in claret and blue.
Also sung by Preston North End fans to taunt Burnley.

Even when we had Moore, Hurst and Peters, West Ham's average finish was about 17th. It just shows how crap the other eight of us were.

Harry Redknapp.

Wimbledon

They have as much charm as a broken beer bottle.

Tommy Docherty.

Football wasn't meant to be run by two linesmen and air traffic control.

Tommy Docherty on Wimbledon's notorious long-ball tactics.

More tea? The Premiership's worst

In our interview with Sir Jack Hayward, the chairman of Wolverhampton Wanderers, page 20, *Sport*, yesterday, we mistakenly attributed to him the following comment: 'Our team was the worst in the First Division and I'm sure it'll be the worst in the Premier League.' Sir Jack had just declined the offer of a hot drink. What he actually said was: 'Our tea was the worst in the First Division and I'm sure it'll be the worst in the Premier League.' Profuse apologies.

The *Guardian*, 12 August 2003.

Silent ground,
Empty ground,
Stolen club,
Plastic town,
Down go Franchise to Division Two,
Take your frenzied supporters with you,
Christ, we hope you go bust;
Christ, we hope you go bust.

Sung by disaffected fans as Wimbledon FC left London for Milton Keynes in 2003, having obtained a 'footballing franchise' there. 'True believers' founded another club – Wimbledon AFC – several leagues lower, which drew bigger crowds.

We're going up, we're going down!

Wimbledon AFC supporters celebrate their new team getting promoted (to Ryman League Division One), as their old one (soon to be Milton Keynes Dons) suffers relegation (to League Division Two); bbc.co.uk, 'Quotes of the Week', April 2004.

■ MEN IN BLACK
the challenging world of the football referee

Who's the wanker,
Who's the wanker,
Who's the wanker in the black?
Universal. To the tune of 'Clementine'.

It's like a toaster, that shirt pocket. Every time there's a tackle, up pops a yellow card.
Kevin Keegan on French referee Joel Quiniou, ITV commentary during Brazil v. USA in the 1994 World Cup.

In all fairness, the referee had a complete cerebral failure.
Footballer Rick Holden. referring to a controversial match between Oldham and Southend, 1995.

I'm trying to be careful what I say, but the referee was useless.
Wolves manager David Jones on Uriah Rennie, 2003.

Even Stevie Wonder would have spotted that one.
Chris Kamara, then Bradford City manager, on David Orr's supposed failure to spot a handball, 1997.

Why is a schoolteacher allowed to control a multi-million pound industry for four or five days every month? After all, the tea lady doesn't roll into a business boardroom at midday and get asked to give the casting vote on a multi-million pound export deal.

An expert view from Jimmy Greaves, 1999.

I felt for the referee. He's is a new, young referee. Sometimes if players don't know the referee they can't say, 'What's your fucking name, you cunt?' If it had been Paul Durkin, they would have said, 'For fuck's sake Paul, Christ Almighty, what sort of fucking decision is that?' And Paul would have said: 'Listen, Roy, fuck off.' The criticism of modern-day referees is that they don't have the character of the referees 10 years ago. That's not the players' fault.

The wisdom of Sir Alex Ferguson, quoted on thewhistler.co.uk, May 2000. The referee in question was Andy d'Urso.

There's a maggot in the golden core of football and it's called the referee.

Danny Baker, 'Six-O-Six', BBC Radio Five Live, on the Chelsea v. Leicester FA Cup replay, 1997, refereed by Mike Reed.

You banker

A preening pompadour, an Emmenthal-eating appeasement monkey...

YOU SWISS BANKER!
Headline in the *Sun*, 25 June 2004, referring to Swiss
referee Urs Meier, whose disallowing of a goal by Sol
Campbell in the last minute of extra time in England's Euro
2004 quarter-final with Portugal consigned England to yet
another major championship defeat in yet another penalty
shoot-out. Meier is in fact a grocer.

**He is Swiss, his name is Urs Meier, and today he is the
most hated man in Britain.**
Valentine Low in the *Evening Standard*, 25 June 2004. Nor
is Meier popular in Romania: in 2003 he received 30,000
abusive e-mails in 36 hours at referee@ursmeier.ch, when
his decision to allow Denmark a 95th minute goal knocked
Romania out of the Euro 2004 qualifiers. The Romanian
newspaper *Pro Sporta* called him a 'Sick Thief', and a coven
of Romanian witches put a curse on him, intended to make
him 'be lame in his legs and feel pain in his soul'.

WHAT AN URS!
Headline in the *Daily Star*, 25 June 2004.

Shame on the Swiss referee, the Emmenthal-eating appeasement monkey who ruined the lives of millions of honest yeomen bearing their simple flag.

Novelist Justin Cartwright in the *Evening Standard*, 25 June 2004.

... a preening pompadour with the looks of a gay porn star.

David Mellor gets personal in the *Evening Standard*, 25 June 2004.

He's the man who put the 'f' in referee. He'd disallow 1945 if he could.

Al Murray (the 'Pub Landlord'), ITV, 26 June 2004.

In Italy, for 30 years under the Borgias, they had warfare, terror, murder and bloodshed, but produced Michelangelo, Leonardo and the Renaissance. In Switzerland they had brotherly love, 500 years of democracy and peace, and what did they produce? Urs Meier.

Ian Chadband in the *Evening Standard*, 2 July 2004.

Big Ron On referees

I never comment on referees and I'm not going to break the habit of a lifetime for that prat.
Ron Atkinson, 1979.

I know where he should have put his flag up, and he'd have got plenty of help.
Ron Atkinson takes issue with the linesman 1996.

If that was a penalty, I'll plait sawdust.
Ron Atkinson, Sheffield Wednesday manager, on Chelsea being awarded a controversial penalty, 1998.

Edvard Munch's *The Scream* incarnate.
Matthew Norman on the startlingly bald Italian referee Pierluigi Collina, in the *Evening Standard*, 14 June 2004.

Referees don't make mistakes. Or at least they don't since I got fined for saying otherwise.

Roma coach Zdenek Zeman, quoted on www.eircom.net.

Then my eyesight started to go, and I took up refereeing.
Neil Midgeley, referee, 1987; quoted in David Pickering, *Cassell's Soccer Companion* (1994).

■ BERKS IN ASTRAKHANS
the all-time great managers

99 per cent of managers who lose their jobs
deserve it.
Mark McGhee, 1996.

The man we want has to fit a certain profile.
Is he a top coach? Would the players respect him?
Is he a nutcase?
David Pleat on the three essentials in a manager, quoted in the *Sunday
Herald*, 2003.

Dick Advocaat

Aptly the Oranje manager is the most Protestant-
looking man of all time. Has the shape of head
crying out to be topped off by a bowler hat.
The *Guardian*, 'Euro 2004: The Definitive Guide', 7 June 2004.

DICK IS A DICK
Banner held up by Dutch fans at the Holland v. Latvia game at Euro 2004.

Sam Allardyce

… the Bolton manager … looks like a butcher. You see him there, chest out on the touchline, and you know he's thinking about loin chops.

'Clogger' in the *Guardian*, 20 August 2001 on the fleshy-jowled Bolton manager.

Ron Atkinson

They call him 'Big Ron' Atkinson because he is a big spender in the transfer market. I just call him 'Fat Ron'.

Malcolm Allison, 1993.

Alan Ball

He's just no good as a manager … We threaten young Stoke fans that Alan Ball will come back and manage the club if they don't go to bed early and eat all their dinner.

Martin Smith, editor of the Stoke City fanzine *The Oatcake*, 1998.

Brian Clough

Old Big Head.

Clough's nickname. Clough himself remarked: 'I call myself Big Head just to remind myself not to be.'

Coaching is for kids. If a player can't trap the ball and pass it by the time he's in the team, he shouldn't be there in the first place. I told Roy McFarland to go and get his bloody hair cut – that's coaching at this level.
Brian Clough in his autobiography, 1994.

He's worse than the rain in Manchester. At least the rain in Manchester stops occasionally.
Bill Shankly on the garrulous Clough, when the latter was manager of Derby County.

Kenny Dalglish

For the benefit of Anglo-Saxon viewers, I wonder if the TV sports presenters would consider using subtitles when interviewing Kenny Dalglish?
Letter to the *Evening Standard*, 1986.

It was very difficult for me to understand what he was saying, which was a pity because there were certain messages I'd have liked to convey to him.
David Ginola, after Dalglish had dispensed with the Frenchman's services at Newcastle United, 1997.

Tommy Docherty

Who would have guessed that behind that arrogant Scots bastard image there lay an arrogant Scots bastard?

Mike Ticher, *When Saturday Comes*, 1986.

All I do know is that I'll never be able to achieve what Tommy Docherty did, and that is take Aston Villa into the third division and Manchester United into the second division.

Ron Atkinson, who also managed both clubs, compares achievements; quoted on www.eircom.net.

Sir Alex Ferguson

A strange bloke, irritated by everyone, I think.

Gary Lineker, 1996.

He's a bloody Scotsman, he shouldn't be part of any élite.

Ken Bates, former Chelsea chairman, on the idea that Sir Alex belongs to 'a New Labour élite'; quoted in the *Evening Standard*, 16 March 2004.

For all his horses, knighthoods and championships, he hasn't got two of what I've got. And I don't mean balls.

Brian Clough on Ferguson's failure to win back-to-back European Cups.

Ouch! Alex and Kenny get personal

Kenny Dalglish has associates but only a few friends. There's nothing wrong with that, as you only need six people to carry your coffin.

Alex Ferguson.

You might as well talk to my baby daughter. You'll get more sense out of her.

Dalglish advises a reporter about to interview Ferguson.

A bully who thinks he is bigger than the game, an erratic old man who has lost his way in the transfer market, selling gold and buying dross … Sir Alex is becoming more and more of a music-hall turn.

David Mellor in the *Evening Standard*, 12 March 2004.

Trevor Francis

Francis could not, in my opinion, spot a great footballer if the bloke's name had four letters in it, started with a P, and ended with an E.

Former England midfielder Alan Hudson, on Birmingham City's new manager, 1997.

Sven the pharmacist

Sophistication without the substance

At last England have appointed a manager who speaks English better than the players.
Brian Clough on the appointment of Eriksson as England coach, quoted on forestfc.co.uk.

We've Sold Our Birthright Down The Fjord To A Nation Of Seven Million Skiers And Hammer Throwers Who Spend Half Their Lives In Darkness.
The *Daily Mail* welcomes the appointment of the Swedish Sven-Göran Eriksson as England manager, 2000.

We needed Winston Churchill and we got ... Ian Duncan Smith.
Anon. England player on Eriksson's half-time team talk during England's 2002 World Cup quarter-final against Brazil, quoted on Radio Five Live, July 2004.

Can we ever trust him again? ... Erik the Eel could still slither off at any time ...
The *Sun*, March 2004, after Eriksson had been 'caught' speaking to Chelsea owner Roman Abramovich.

... we have invested so much in our perception of Sven the Guru that Sven the Doofus is an inconceivable idea. Yet he was a doofus against France. A solid gold, 24-carat, 100 per cent doofus.

Martin Samuel in *The Times*, 16 June 2004, blames Sven for England's 2–1 defeat to France in Euro 2004. Samuel commented: 'Eriksson took Wayne Rooney off, put Heskey on and that decision cost the game. It was his Ranieri moment.'

You look at Sven and you think ... he's a pharmacist ... he should be saying, 'Here's your pile ointment.'

Frank Skinner, *Fantasy Football*, ITV, 25 June 2004.

That man is supposed to be a Viking, and he defends!

Al Murray, ITV, 26 June 2004. The 'Pub Landlord' inveighs against Swedish Sven's defensive tactics in Euro 2004: 'We should have been raping and pillaging the Portuguese.'

He has the aura of sophistication but not the substance.

David Walsh in *The Sunday Times*, 28 June 2004.

He is what John Major would be if he swallowed a bucket of Viagra.

Paul Hayward in the *Daily Telegraph*, 6 August 2004, following revelations that Sven, along with FA chief executive Mark Palios, had had an affair with an FA secretary Faria Alam.

Barry Fry

Someone once said you could write down Barry's knowledge of management on a postage stamp. I would say you need to fold the stamp in half.

Former Birmingham City striker Steve Claridge, 1997.

George Graham

OUT ON HIS ARSENAL

Headline in the *Daily Star* after George Graham was sacked as Arsenal manager, 1995.

Q: What's the difference between George Graham and British tennis players?
A: George Graham can return backhanders.

The Onion Bag, 1995.

Ruud Gullit

A part-time playboy manager who carried out his lucrative commercial contracts at the expense of his training.

Chelsea chairman Ken Bates explains why the manager was sacked in 1998.

He thinks he is God and we are all nobodies.

Christina Gullit, his estranged wife, 1998.

Glenn Hoddle

If Glenn Hoddle is right then I must have been a failed football manager in a previous existence.

Blind Labour politician David Blunkett, 1999, on the England manager's assertion that people born with disabilities were being punished for their past sins through the working out of karma 'from another lifetime'. Hoddle's words were 'You and I have been physically given two hands and two legs and half-decent brain. Some people have not been born like that for a reason. The karma is working from another lifetime. It is not only people with disabilities. What you sow you have to reap.' Hoddle was duly sacked.

If his theory is correct, he is in for real problems in the next life. He will probably be doomed to come back as Glenn Hoddle.

Sports minister Tony Banks MP, 1999.

Hoddle 0, Disabled 1 (Hoddle o.g.)

Headline in the *Independent* reporting Hoddle's sacking by the FA.

Jesus was a normal, run-of-the-mill sort of guy who had a genuine gift, just as Eileen has.

Glenn Hoddle on his faith healer friend Eileen Drewery, 1998.

Too many times he has used his role to promote his beliefs as a supermarket hippy.

The verdict of Italian newspaper *Gazzetta dello Sport*.

NOT WANTED – DEAD OR ALIVE

Placard held up by a Southampton fan as rumours circulated of a Hoddle return as Southampton manager, February 2004.

If he were an ice-cream he'd lick himself.

Unidentified player, quoted by Simon Hughes in the *Daily Telegraph*, 16 February 2004.

Gerard Houllier

Potless and clueless.

'Clogger' in the *Guardian*, 24 February 2004.

Kevin Keegan

According to *The Express*, Kevin Keegan will star in an advertising campaign aimed at tempting people back to Church this Christmas. Presumably Keggy was hired because of the way his Euro 2000 team inspired 20 million watching Englishmen to shout 'Jesus Christ!' in unison.

'Mediawatch', Football365.com.

A big baby who deserves the sack.

Former Manchester City player Eyal Berkovic on Kevin Keegan as manager of Manchester City, quoted in the *Evening Standard*, 23 January 2004.

Volcanic managers

To describe his anger as volcanic is plainly inadequate … He makes Gordon Ramsay sound like the Maharishi Mahesh Yogi.

Chris Maume in the *Independent*, 10 July 2004.

Put 'Graeme Souness + bust-up' into the Google search engine, and 2,170 entries come up in 0.29 seconds.

Matthew Norman on Souness the manager, in the *Evening Standard*, 22 March 2004.

Brian Kidd

What the gaffer [Sir Alex Ferguson] saw in me, I don't know. I asked him once: 'Why me?' He just started laughing and I haven't asked him since.

Brian Kidd on being assistant manager at Manchester United, 1998.

Jose Mourinho

A youthful Perry Como.

Ken Dyer on Chelsea's new Portuguese manager, in the *Evening Standard*, 5 July 2004.

Who do you think you are having meetings about me? You were a crap player and you are a crap manager. The only reason I have dealings with you is that somehow you are the manager of my country and you're not even Irish, you English cunt… Stick it up your bollocks.

The 'highly motivated' Roy Keane has a few quiet words with the Republic of Ireland national team manager, Yorkshireman Mick McCarthy, May 2002. Keane was sent home by McCarthy before the start of the 2002 World Cup when a team meeting intended to clear the air ended with Keane launching the above tirade of abuse at his bemused manager. The *Guardian* commented: 'Keane's remark will long be remembered by students of anatomy.'

David O'Leary

I would rather gouge my eyes out with a rusty spoon than have O'Leary back.

Leeds United Independent Fans' Association founder Simon Jose reacts to reports that the former manager is set to return, 'Quotes of the week', bbc.co.uk, November 2003.

Dreary O'Leary.

David Mellor in the *Evening Standard*, 23 April 2004.

David Pleat

David Pleat ... chose to rise from his dug-out, just as Spurs fans were chanting: 'Stand up if you want Pleat out'.

'Quotes of the Week, on bbc.co.uk, 10 May 2004.

The man is mad; certifiably, eye-spinningly mad.

Danny Kelly on Tottenham Hotspur's 'director of football', Talk Radio, 1998.

Claudio Ranieri

TINKBOMB

Headline in the *Sun*, 21 April 2004.

The Tinkerman made some crazy substitutions? So, the Pope's Catholic.

David Mellor in the *Evening Standard*, 23 April 2004, after Ranieri's substitutions had turned Chelsea's 1–0 lead into a 1–3 defeat by Monaco in the Champions League semi-final.

What the fuck was that about?

Anonymous Chelsea player, presumably English, after the Monaco match.

Alas, poor Claudio ...
You're being sacked in the summer!

Charlton Athletic fans taunt Ranieri, who shouted back the correction, 'No, I will be sacked in May!'; quoted on bbc.co.uk, 2004.

Dead man walking.

Ranieri's description of himself, 2003–04 season, when it became apparent that Chelsea's owner and chairman were determined to appoint a new manager.

Harry Redknapp

A second-rate huckster.

Matthew Norman in the *Evening Standard*, 2004.

Peter Reid

Cheer up Peter Reid,
Oh what can it mean …
He sent Sunderland down
And now he's trying with Leeds …

Sung by West Ham fans (to the tune of the Monkees' 'Daydream Believer') during a game with Leeds.

Peter Reid: Down-to-earth Scouser, who remains untouched by the suave sophistication of his continental managerial colleagues.

The Times, 16 June 2004.

Sir Bobby Robson

His natural expression is that of a man who fears he has left the gas on.

David Lacey of the *Guardian* on Robson as England manager during the 1980s.

Steve Sampson

When we're old we'll have scrapbooks, but hopefully the most important thing is the respect of the people you're associated with. Steve is going to have to settle for a scrapbook.

US defender Alexei Lalas on being left out of the 1998 World Cup squad by US coach Steve Sampson.

Jacques Santini

Jacques Santini could do nothing with the world's best players. So he's perfect for Spurs then.

Ian Chadband on the Tottenham-bound former manager of France (who were eliminated by Greece in the Euro 2004 quarter-finals); in the *Evening Standard*, 2 July 2004.

Jacques Santini ... turning France into Spurs rather than Spurs into France.

Michael Walker in the *Guardian*. 6 July 2004, quotes a joke popular at Euro 2004.

Luiz Felipe Scolari

Appearance: Ken Livingstone on a strict gammon, chips and taste-the-difference mayonnaise diet.

The *Guardian*, 'Euro 2004: The Definitive Guide'; on Portugal's coach, 7 June 2004. For most commentators 'Big Phil' resembled US actor Gene Hackman.

Come on Motivating the lads

I've told the players we need to win so that I can have the cash to buy some new ones.

Peterborough United manager Chris Turner before a Littlewoods Cup quarter-final, 1992.

Graham Taylor

As well as being England's first managerial turnip, Graham Taylor has Prime Ministerial qualities, combining the personality of John Major with the gift of prophecy of Neville Chamberlain.

Steve Grant, *Time Out*, 1994.

Phil Thompson

Sit down Pinocchio, sit down Pinocchio...

Fans taunt Liverpool's large-snouted assistant manager, to the tune of 'La donna é mobile' from Giuseppe Verdi's opera *Rigoletto*.

Get your nostrils,
Get your nostrils,
Get your nostrils off the pitch …

And again …, to the tune of *Cwm Rhondda*.

Terry Venables

Unfit to be concerned in any way with the management of a company.

Elizabeth Gloster QC, as the former England manager and serial entrepreneur was banned from company directorship for 7 years in 1998.

Gianluca Vialli

You wouldn't trust a learner driver with a Formula One car.

Former Milan coach Fabio Capello on Vialli's appointment as Chelsea manager, 1998.

Berti Vogts

If he doesn't jump soon he runs the risk of being the most unpopular visitor to Scotland since Rudolf Hess crash-landed.

'Clogger' in the *Guardian*, 24 February 2004, on Scotland's German manager, following Scotland's 3–0 loss to Wales.

■ ENGLAND, 1966–2004
(mainly 2004, in fact)

Ultimately the real loser in 1966 was English football. [Sir Alf] Ramsey's success reinforced English insularity and reduced what willingness there was to learn from abroad, thus condemning the national game to the status of a backwater.

David Downing on England's 1966 World Cup final victory, in *The Best of Enemies: England v Germany* (2000).

Yurrrgggggh!!! Der stod Ingelland!!! Lord Nelson!!! Lord Beaverbrook!!! Winston Churchill!!! Henry Cooper!!! Clement Attlee!!! Anthony Eden!!! Lady Diana!!! Der stod dem all!!! Der stod dem all!!! Maggie Thatcher, can you hear me? Can you hear me, Maggie? Your boys took one hell of a beating tonight!!!

Borg Lillelien, Norwegian commentator, is transported by the scoreline Norway 2, England 1, 1981.

When I played I always loved to go out against English teams because they always gave you the ball back if you lost it. They still do.

Johann Cruyff, former Ajax and Netherlands captain, 1998.

World Cup 1986

The goal was scored a little bit by the hand of God, a little by the head of Maradona.

For the English football fan, perhaps the ultimate insult. Diego Maradona crows about the goal he fisted into the England net in the 1986 World Cup quarter-final when Argentina's 2–1 victory put England out of the competition.

Swedes 2 Turnips 1

Spanish 1 Onions 0

Norse manure

Yanks 2 Planks 0

Sun headlines on English defeats by, respectively, Sweden, Spain, Norway and the USA under the management of Graham Taylor, 1992–3, when England failed to qualify for the 1994 World Cup. The *Sun* famously reacted by the national team's failure by publishing a photograph of Taylor with a turnip for a head (see page 106).

I don't like English football – running, fighting, war for 90 minutes without a break. I prefer a more intelligent game, holding up the ball and playing. For me, Germany is more like home.

Former Leeds United striker Tony Yeboah moves to Hamburg, 1999.

World Cup 1990

There's probably a space probe circling Earth still looking for the ball that Chris Waddle launched into the stratosphere from the penalty spot.

Ben Woolhead on Chris Waddle's penalty shootout miss that condemned England to defeat in the 1990 World Cup semi-final against Germany; in 'I Love the 90s' on www.stylusmagazine.com.

Ingerland   The fans abroad

Brainless, senseless, sacks of beer. The only thing they represent is brutish stupidity in its purest form, with gratuitous violence and a desire to destroy other people as their only means of expression.

Editorial in the French newspaper *Libération*, describing England fans at the 1998 World Cup.

Imbeciles whose bestial violence and squalid alcoholism have deprived them of the tiniest ounce of humanity.

Editorial in *La Marseillaise*, 1998.

World Cup 1998

Before the 1998 World Cup, there was a theory going round that England would win the World Cup, based upon the following palindromic 'proof':

1966 England
1970 Brazil
1974 Germany
1978 Argentina
1982 Italy
1986 Argentina
1990 Germany
1994 Brazil
1998 England ???

The originators of that theory have re-examined this proof and have come up with an equally palindromic proof which clearly shows why England didn't win:

1970 Won fuck all
1974 Won fuck all
1978 Won fuck all
1982 Won fuck all
1986 Won fuck all
1990 Won fuck all
1994 Won fuck all
1998 Won fuck all

The Tartan Army home page, on www.t-army.com.

World Cup 2002

Sven-Göran Eriksson's inability to change the tactics against Brazil changed the Friday morning atmosphere in school halls across the nation from carnival to double maths.

Martin Kelner on Sven's first major championship failure: England's 1–2 World Cup quarter-final defeat by Brazil; in the *Guardian*, 1 July 2002.

All you have to do is find a bunch of nobodies – a team filled with players that not even Harry Redknapp would buy – and England are in disarray.

Simon Barnes in *The Times*, 18 June 2004.

Watching England in a major tournament is like having a fry-up three times a day from the age of five.

Paul Hayward on the stresses of watching England; the *Daily Telegraph*, 25 June 2004.

… [England's] tactics … made George Graham's Arsenal look like Pelé's Brazil.

Matthew Norman in the *Evening Standard*, 14 June 2004, on England's tactics in their 2–1 defeat to France at Euro 2004.

England cannot be guaranteed to have won any match until at least five minutes after the final whistle has sounded.

Pete Clark in the *Evening Standard*, 14 June 2004, after England conceded two goals in extra time to squander a 1–0 lead over France, Euro 2004.

Well done Helder, the potatoes always taste better after you have eaten the beef!

Portuguese hamburger advert, June 2004 featuring Portugal and Tottenham striker Helder Postiga eating chips. Postiga was the scorer of an equaliser and a cheeky penalty in his country's quarter-final defeat of England at Euro 2004, and in Portuguese '*bifes*' is a slang term for English people.

… shoot-out duds of the international game.

James Lawton in the *Independent*, 25 June 2004, after England lost to Portugal on penalties in the quarter-finals of Euro 2004.

GO HOME – TRY CRICKET

Swiss banner at England v. Switzerland, Euro 2004.

They have given us over the years a series of performances that have had the nation hiding behind the national sofa while Norwegians gloat and the San Marinese stand up and cheer. England could have beaten Brazil and should have beaten France: you wonder if they would be capable of winning promotion from the Conference.

Simon Barnes in *The Times*, 18 June 2004.

... football has come home – through the tradesman's entrance at Luton airport.

Martin Kelner welcomes the England boys after their quarter-final exit from Euro 2004, in the *Guardian*, 2 July 2004.

Wayne's World

Sights and sounds of Euro 2004

A trio of lobster-pink fat men bouncing up and down yelling 'Rooo-neeeee'.

Steven Gerrard spitting profusely as the commentator uses the phrase 'the beautiful game'.

Sven reacting to an England goal by joyfully adjusting his glasses.

Gary Neville being described as 'very much the unsung hero' for the 73rd time.

David James wearing the perplexed expression of a dog trying to work out how to use a can-opener as the ball nestles in the goals behind him.

Someone using the phrase 'Wayne's World'.

From Harry Pearson, 'Count those clichés with a spotter's log', in the *Guardian*, 24 June 2004.

■ ABUSE SANS FRONTIÈRES
the international scene

I left a couple of my foreigners out last week and they started talking in 'foreign'. I knew what they were saying: 'blah, blah, blah, le b****** manager, f****** useless b******!'

Portsmouth manager Harry Redknapp, on 'Quotes of the Week', bbc.co.uk, March 2004.

 **A view from north of the border**

Reporter: Gordon, do you think James Beattie deserves to be in the England squad?

Strachan: I don't care. I'm Scottish.

Lineker: So Gordon, if you were English, what formation would you play?

Strachan: If I was English, I'd top myself!

Southampton manager Gordon Strachan.

Argentina

Bangers with Batistuta and cornflakes with Crespo!

Possibly an insult, certainly John Motson at his most hysterical. BBC TV
commentary on England v. Argentina during the group stages of the 2002
World Cup, won 1–0 by England with a Beckham penalty.

Why the surprise at Argentina going out? When
did a team with a large Scottish following ever
qualify for the second round of a World Cup?

Andy Trollope, letter inspired by Argentina's early exit from the 2002 World
Cup, quoted in the *Guardian*, 1 July 2002.

China

You would think if any team could put up a decent
wall it would be China.

Terry Venables on China's feeble defending against free kicks in the 2002
World Cup, quoted in the *Guardian*, 1 July 2002.

 **Why Brazil have won only
five World Cups**

There were great players there, but they were terribly
indisciplined. Their antics would not have been
tolerated in Scotland.

Archie Maclean, Scottish footballer who moved to Brazil in
1912, quoted in Alex Bellos, *Futebol* (2002).

France

So inept … it should have been the biggest national scandal since a glass pyramid was shoved outside the Louvre.

Ian Chadband on France's defeat by Greece in the Euro 2004 quarter-finals; in the *Evening Standard*, 2 July 2004.

Germany

It must be possible to find 30 excellent football players among 80 million people.

Egidius Braun, President of the German FA, on the state of the national team in the 1998 World Cup.

If you put all the German players in a sack and hit it, you would get someone who deserved it.

German legend Franz Beckenbauer on Germany's unconvincing 1–0 win over the USA in the 2002 World Cup; quoted in the *Guardian*, 1 July 2002.

You have to, you know, to some degree, er, admire them …

Former England manager Bobby Robson on Germany's overachieving 2002 World Cup squad which somehow contrived to reach the final.

… Lederhosen and Bratwurst … players who look like Hamburg taxi drivers and porn stars.

Richard Williams in the *Guardian*, 16 June 2004; on what he fears may be the type of German team at Euro 2004.

England v. Germany

The best of enemies

What wonderful goals. You really ought to get a closer look at them.

British ambassador Sir Neville Henderson offers Hermann Goering his binoculars during Germany's 3–6 home defeat by England, 14 May 1938; quoted in David Downing, *The Best of Enemies: England v Germany* (2000).

Two World Wars and one World Cup,
Doo-dah, doo-dah,
Two World Wars and one World Cup,
Doo-dah-doo-dah day ...

A post-1966 favourite of England fans (when not humming the theme from *The Great Escape*).

Help our boys clout the Krauts.

The Sun, before England's World Cup semi-final against Germany, 1990, a match England lost in a penalty shoot-out.

If their football was as bad as their sense of humour they wouldn't be in the World Cup.

Bernard Manning sulks after England's defeat, 1990.

LET'S BLITZ FRITZ!

Headline in the *Sun* newspaper before the England v. Germany semi-final in Euro 1996. The *Sun* had earlier instructed its readers to 'treat our European guests with respect and affection'.

Why do you look like freshly cooked lobsters after one day on the beach?

The German tabloid newspaper *Bild* responds to German-bashing English tabloid headlines during Euro 1996, June 1996.

HUN-NIL!

The *Sunday People* greets England's 1–0 defeat of Germany in Euro 2000.

DON'T MENTION THE SCORE!

Headline in both the *Independent on Sunday* and the *News of the World* (echoing Basil Fawlty's 'Don't mention the war!'), greets England's 5–1 defeat of Germany in a World Cup qualifying game, 1 September 2001. The result was greeted with ecstasy in England and disbelief in Germany, the German goalkeeper Oliver Kahn remarking: ' ... this result was shameful. You could just as well have put a sports bag in goal ... There will be scars for life.' Quotes of the Year, *Guardian Weekend*, 29 December 2001.

Oh go on then, mention the war ...

Germany, not for the first time this century, invading Czech territory.
Ron Atkinson, commentating on the 1996 European Championship final.

My grandfather wants his bicycle back.
Football chant sung by Dutch fans at Holland v. Germany matches. The occupying Germans systematically confiscated Dutch bicycles during World War II.

... a dreadful travesty of the memory of Franz Beckenbauer.
Richard Williams in the *Guardian*, 16 June 2004; commenting on an error by Jens Nowotny during Germany's match with Holland, Euro 2004.

RUDI, WIR SIND DIE DEPPEN EUROPAS
(Rudi, we are the idiots of Europe)
Bild newspaper headline as Germany follow Spain and Italy out of Euro 2004 at the group stages after losing 2–1 to the Czech Republic. 'Lufthansa will be one busy airline this morning,' commented the *Guardian*. Manager Rudi Völler resigned after the defeat.

The Germans are out – that's the main thing.
Al Murray (the Pub Landlord), 26 June 2004, following England's quarter-final exit from Euro 2004 (the Germany having exited at the group stages).

A song for Europe

Greece

Greece are to major tournaments what Humpty Dumpty was to King's horses and all the King's men – nothing but a minor irritant which self-destructs on request... They are officially the second-worst team ever to have played a World Cup.
The *Guardian* 'Euro 2004: The Definitive Guide', 7 June 2004. The 100–1 outsiders, who had never won a match in any previous competition, duly flabbergasted everyone by winning the tournament.

A meaningless clash of confusing alphabets.
The *Guardian* 'Euro 2004: The Definitive Guide', looks forward to the Greece v. Russia tie at the group stages, 7 June 2004.

... football? Bloody Hellas!
George Caulkin in *The Times*, parodying the words of Alex Ferguson (see page 12), greets Greece's victory in Euro 2004, 5 July 2004.

The biggest thing to hit Greece since Demis Roussos.

Gary Lineker on Greece's defeat of Portugal to win Euro 2004, BBC TV, 4 July 2004.

Hungary

Look at that little fat chap there ... we'll murder this lot!

Unnamed England player on the great Ferenc Puskas, before a match in 1953 that Hungary won 6–3, quoted in David Pickering, *Cassell's Soccer Companion* (1994).

Ireland

If you have a fortnight's holiday in Dublin you qualify for an Eire cap.

Mike England, 1986, quoted in *The Guinness Book of Humorous Sports Quotes* (1996).

A true football fan is one who knows the nationality of every player in the Republic of Ireland team.

Ken Bolam, musician, on the effect of the 'granny qualification', 1996.

Italy

Catenaccio: a word used by Brian Glanville to demonstrate his knowledge of Italian football. Its meaning can be loosely translated as 'bribery'.

When Saturday Comes, 1986.

If they speak about corruption, it must be because they are used to practising it.

Ecuadorian referee Byron Moreno, the target of hate-mail from Italy after he sent off Italy's star striker Francesco Totti in Italy's 2–1 second-round defeat by tournament co-hosts South Korea, hits back at his Italian critics; quoted in the *Guardian*, 1 July 2002.

 **The homesickness of the long-distance Scouser**

I couldn't settle in Italy – it was like living in a foreign country.

Former Liverpool striker Ian Rush, reflecting on his spell at Juventus.

Norway

Yes, fuck off.

Paul Gascoigne, when asked on television if he had a message for the people of Norway.

Sing when you're whaling,
You only sing when you're whaling ...

Sung by Scottish fans to Norwegian fans during the 1998 World Cup
('Guantanamera' again).

Scotland

ALCOHOLISM v COMMUNISM

Banner waved by Scottish fans during a game versus the USSR, 1982.

This is an unusual Scotland side because they have good players.

Javier Clemente, Spanish coach, on Scotland's 1996 Under-21 side, on
www.eircom.net.

Unless we can find a McRonaldo or a Hamish Zidane, we'll have to go with what we've got.

Craig Brown, Scotland manager, looks forward to the 1998 World Cup.

Spain

Every time a major tournament begins, they turn up with a formidable squad and the cliché that it 'may be their turn' is wheeled out. And every time they slink away, having found a perplexing way to lose to a palpably inferior side.

Matthew Norman in the *Evening Standard*, 21 June 2004.

Switzerland

Secretive hoarders of Nazi gold and dictators' nest eggs make feelings of sympathy downright impossible.

The *Guardian*, 'Switzerland's mountain scapegoats', 18 June 2004, after England's 3–0 defeat of Switzerland in Euro 2004.

USA

Even if we lose, we will take to the streets – we'll just chant 'Death to America' instead.

16-year-old Iranian Amir Khosro on the USA v. Iran tie in the 1998 World Cup: www.eircom.net.

Wales

Mrs Merton: Is it your ambition to get sent off in a World Cup Final?

Vinnie Jones: I play for Wales.

The *Mrs Merton Show*, BBC TV, 1997.

■ HACKS AND MOTORMOUTHS

I've always said there's a place for the press, but they haven't dug it yet.
Tommy Docherty, 1980.

Hello my sharks – welcome to the funeral.
Chelsea manager Claudio Ranieri greets the press before the Champions' League semi-final second leg with Monaco, May 2004.

Ron Atkinson

Regius Professor of Cliché at the University of All Fairness (formerly To Be Fair Polytechnic).
Matthew Norman, *Evening Standard*, 29 March 2004.

Part of Big Ron's appeal was his quaint mangling of the English language, an argot all his own that was dubbed Ronglish.
Martin Kelner in 'Euro 2004: The Definitive Guide', the *Guardian*, 7 June 2004.

The Great Unmentionable.
David Lopati in a letter to *The Times*, 16 June 2004. Unmentionable because of his regrettable description of Marcel Desailly (see box on page 127).

Big Ron's boobs   Is that on?

He's a little twat, that Totti. I can't see what all the fuss is about.
Ron Atkinson, unaware that his microphone is still on, after AS Roma v. Arsenal, ITV, November 2002. His journalistic career survived.

He is what is known in some schools as a fucking lazy thick n*****.
Ron Atkinson, ITV, again unaware that his microphone is still on, after Monaco v. Chelsea, 20 April 2004, referring to Marcel Desailly. This time he lost his ITV commentating job and his *Guardian* column.

Trevor Brooking

England's most cultured ex-midfielder and now leading BBC television barbiturate … he still manages to make Nigel Mansell sound like Murray Walker on acid. And he looks like Virginia Wade.
Zit magazine, 1993.

David Coleman

Anything that matters so much to David Coleman, you realize doesn't matter so much at all.
Clive James in the *Observer*, 1978.

Jimmy Greaves

A walrus in a woolly jumper … as illuminating as the average taxi driver, without the saving grace of getting you anywhere.

Victor Lewis-Smith on the footballer-turned-pundit, *Evening Standard*, 1992.

Alan Hansen

Thunderbirds puppet who's now made a career out of bleating on and on about Liverpool's injury problems on Match of the Day …

Zit, 1993.

Emlyn Hughes

Conjugate the verb 'done great': I done great. He done great. We done great. They done great. The boy Lineker done great.

Letter to the *Guardian*, 1986, on the World Cup commentating of former England players Emlyn Hughes and Mike Channon.

Chris Kamara

Born to shout, Kamara is Sid [Waddell] without the classical education, the Geordie patois and the surreal wit, but with a moustache.

Giles Smith *on* Sky Sports Nationwide League match summarizer Chris Kamara, in *The Times*, 20 May 2004.

Radio football

> Radio football is the game reduced to its lowest
> common denominator. Shorn of the game's aesthetic
> pleasures … or the sense of security you get from
> seeing that your defenders and goalkeeper are more or
> less where they should be, all that is left is naked fear.
> Nick Hornby in *Fever Pitch* (1992).

… reporting on events that will not … be
troubling the headline writers for the next day's
papers … he will be talking as if strapped to the
radiator grille of a terrorist truck-bomb hurtling
towards a building of serious significance.
Giles Smith on Kamara's commentating style, again.

… the irate gargle of a hyena that has just been
shot in the buttocks.
Giles Smith again.

Mark Lawrenson

When was the last time you were mistaken for a
German porn star?
Question put to Lawrenson in 'First and Last', *Observer Sports Monthly*,
6 June 2004.

Gary Lineker

Alan Hansen and Gary Lineker are Mr and Mrs Mogadon.
Zit magazine, 1993.

There is something of the crisp salesman about this fellow that is difficult to eradicate from the mind.
Pete Clark in the *Evening Standard*: 'Euro 2004: The Ultimate Guide'.

Des Lynam Half man, half moustache

The Leslie Phillips of sports broadcasting.
Martin Kelner in the *Guardian*.

... a mythical creature ... half man, half moustache.
Martin Kelner in 'Euro 2004: The Definitive Guide', the *Guardian* 7 June 2004.

The Roger Moore of sports presenters: his idea of emotion is to raise an eyebrow.
Jim Bush, letter to *The Times*, 2 July 2004.

A smug chimera of Dickie Davis and Terry-Thomas.
Tim Baker, letter to *The Times*, 2 July 2004.

He sits like an old package of St Agur in your fridge. You're never quite sure if he's finally gone off.
Ashley Head, letter to *The Times*, 2 July 2004.

As a piece of music, it's dog's piss.
Noel Gallagher on the *Match of the Day* signature tune,
BBC TV, 8 August 2004.

Gabby Logan

Just like the other Totti, Gabby should be banned
from the rest of the tournament.
Letter to *The Times*, June 2004. The Italian Totti had received a ban for
spitting during Euro 2004.

Ally McCoist

Chirpy studio Lothario who is always eager to
please, with a cheeky grin and a really bad joke,
whatever the state of the match.
The Times, 16 June 2004.

David Mellor

I can only assume that callers to Six-O-Six
repeatedly ask David Mellor how he is on the off-
chance that he will one day reply 'Terminally ill'.
Letter to *When Saturday Comes*, 1999.

John Motson

His career could only really be enhanced by a laryngectomy.

Matthew Norman in the *Evening Standard*, 1994.

… football trivia … blows like a gale through his brain.

Evening Standard, 22 June 2004.

Jonathan Pearce

He makes Michelle from Pop Idol look like Gandhi on the Atkins Diet.

Matthew Norman on BBC Radio Five's ample commentator Jonathan Pearce; in the *Evening Standard* 22 March 2004. Norman described Pearce's style of commentary as 'screaming … like a psychotic town crier'.

 Tweedledum and Tweedledumber

Two men whose self-regard is even larger than their stomachs … two low-rent egomaniacs … the Tweedledum and Tweedledumber of sports broadcasting.

Matthew Norman on Radio Five's heavyweight football commentators Alan Green and Jonathan Pearce, *Evening Standard*, 22 March 2004.

Gordon! Strachan 1, Hacks 0

Reporter: Gordon, can we have a quick word please?

Strachan: Velocity. (Walks off)

Reporter: Gordon, you must be delighted with that result?

Strachan: You're spot on! You can read me like a book.

Reporter: This might seem like a daft question, but you'll be happy to get your first win under your belt, won't you?

Strachan: You're right, it is a daft question. I'm not even going to bother answering that one. It is a daft question, you're spot on there.

Reporter: There's no negative vibes or negative feelings here?

Strachan: Apart from yourself, we're all quite positive round here. I'm going to whack you round the head with a big stick. Down, negative man, down.

Assorted exchanges with the former Southampton manager Gordon Strachan, recorded on The Motley Fool.co.uk and bbc.co.uk.

Radio drone-in

Eminent wireless historians estimate that, in the 36 years since Radio Nottingham broadcast the first phone-in in 1968, no more than 12 good points have been made within the genre. Only one of these was in a sport phone-in.

Marina Hyde, *The Guardian*, April 2004.

Clive Tyldesley

No lightness of touch, devoid of wit, absolutely no self-deprecation and his opinions on matters of fact are unfailingly deluded. Out.

Tyldesley is voted out of *The Times*'s 'Big Bother' studio of Euro 2004 commentators for premature celebration of an England victory before Zidane's double strike in England's match with France; letter to *The Times*, 16 June 2004.

Bring on the trainer, it looks like he's strained a metaphor.

Paul Jesperson, letter to *The Times*, 16 June 2004.

Bob Wilson

He just about sums Arsenal up – the verbal equivalent of a square pass along the back four.

Bob Wilson, former Arsenal goalkeeper and presenter of *Football Focus* on BBC TV, as seen by *When Saturday Comes*.

■ THE FAT CATS

The ideal Board of Directors should be made up of three men – two dead and one dying.
Tommy Docherty, 1977.

Football hooligans? Well, there are 92 club chairmen for a start.
Brian Clough, 1980.

You could put his knowledge of the game on a postage stamp. He wanted us to sign Salford Van Hire because he thought he was a Dutch international.
Fred Ayre on an unnamed Wigan Athletic director, 1981; quoted in David Pickering, *Cassell's Soccer Companion* (1994).

I have found Alan Sugar to be one of the least charming people I have ever come across.
Strong words for an Arsenal chairman. Peter Hill-Wood on his Spurs counterpart, 1997.

The trouble with Al-Fayed is that he doesn't understand British traditions and institutions. I mean, he took over Fulham and made them successful.
Andy Hamilton, BBC Radio 4, *News Quiz*, 1999.

Ron II — Kick Noadism out of sport!

The black players at this club lend the side a lot of skill and flair, but you also need white players to balance things up and give the team some brains and common sense.

Ron Noades, chairman of Crystal Palace, 1991.

Richardson is the type who would trample a two-year-old child to pick up a 2p piece.

South Yorkshire police officer Ian Marshall on the former Doncaster Rovers owner Ken Richardson, who burned the club's stand down for the insurance money, 1999.

On hearing that Chelsea fans wished him to be replaced as Chelsea chairman by Matthew Harding:

So what? Ninety-nine per cent of all Iraqis voted for Saddam Hussein.

Ken Bates, 1995.

Abramovich knows nothing about football.

Chelsea manager Claudio Ranieri's assessment of Chelsea's Russian owner Roman Abramovich , 'Quotes of the Week', bbc.co.uk, April 2004.

The Average Director's Knowledge of Football

Chapter heading in the autobiography of Sunderland legend Len Shackleton. The chapter itself was a blank page.

Ken Bates: all the elegance, insight and wit of a mildly retarded pub landlord.

Matthew Norman in the *Evening Standard*, 16 February 2003, on Ken Bates's notorious Chelsea programme notes.

Ken Bates was accused of being many things while he was the chairman of Chelsea: arrogant, abrasive, evasive, cantankerous, ruthless, heartless, egotistical, greedy, secretive, self-serving and deluded. He also had his bad points.

The *Independent*, 25 March 2004.

A footballing cretin.

Celtic manager Martin O'Neill on Ken Bates, quoted in the *Daily Telegraph*, 27 March 2004.

£££ **Support from the chairman ...**

I met with the manager on Tuesday night specifically to sack him. We had a lengthy meeting to discuss compensation. The amount agreed, it transpired, could not be funded by the Board. So basically we could not afford to sack him. I have now given the manager my full support.

David Taylor, chairman of Huddersfield Town, gets right behind manager Mick Wadsworth; quoted on www.eircom.net.

■ FOOTBALLING CHAUVINISM
a short survey

Women should be in the kitchen, the discotheque and the boutique, but not in football.

Ron Atkinson, 1989. Quoted in David Pickering, *Cassell's Soccer Companion* (1994).

It hit me half-way through my stag night that I'd rather be going to the match than marry Nicola.

Hereford United fan Kevin McCall, who cancelled his wedding in 1991 rather than miss a match, quoted in David Pickering, *Cassell's Soccer Companion* (1994).

It was a girls' night out.

Bolton striker John McGinley on a mass brawl during a Bolton v. Manchester United match, 1997.

Cup sizes A fair comparison

... the League Cup ... Dannii Minogue to the FA Cup's Kylie ...

Matthew Norman, in the *Evening Standard*, 1 March 2004.

Thanks very much and let's have coffee

To put it in gentleman's terms, if you've been out for a night and you're looking for a young lady and you pull one, you've done what you set out to do. We didn't look our best today but we've pulled. Some weeks the lady is good looking and some weeks they're not. Our performance today would have been not the best- looking bird but at least we got her in the taxi. She may not have been the best-looking lady we ended up taking home but it was still very pleasant and very nice, so thanks very much and let's have coffee.

QPR manager Ian Holloway on his team's limp performance against Chesterfield, 'Quotes of the Year, 2003', on bbc.co.uk.

I knew it wasn't going to be our day when I found out we had a woman running the line. She should be at home making the tea or the dinner for her man after he has been to the football. This is a professional man's game.

Albion Rovers manager Peter Hetherston on referee Morag Pirie. He later resigned.

Newcastle girls are all dogs.

Newcastle United directors Freddie Shepherd and Doug Hall to a *News of the World* investigative reporter, 1998.

Handbags.

Universal term, possibly coined by Ron Atkinson, for any on-pitch outbreak of childish behaviour.

Hi babe, my name's Mick Quinn. You look wonderful. I was just wondering whether you fancied a shag?

Quinn tries it on with Miss World in a Newcastle club; quoted in his autobiography, *Who Ate All the Pies* (2003). Miss World did not speak English.

I don't know what the fuss is all about. They're all ugly.

Czech player Vratislav Lokvenc, alleged remark to Czech journalists after sharing a hotel with the England players' wives and girlfriends, Quoted by Matt Lawton in the *Daily Mail*, 5 July 2004.

Cricket

Baseball on Valium

Personally, I have always looked on cricket as organised loafing.

Future archbishop of Canterbury William Temple, addressing parents when he was headmaster of Repton, *c.*1914.

I guess this homo business started earlier than I thought.

Groucho Marx, on being shown a painting of an early cricket match in the Long Room at Lords.

It requires one to assume such indecent postures.

Oscar Wilde explains his aversion to cricket.

Hit-and-giggle   One-day cricket

For six days, thou shall push up and down the line, but on the seventh day thou shall swipe.
Doug Padgett, Yorkshire cricketer 1969, on the early days of Sunday League cricket.

A test match is like a painting. A one-day match is like a Rolf Harris painting.
Former Australian captain Ian Chappell.

When's the game itself going to begin?
Groucho Marx again, whilst watching a match at Lord's.

I have seen cricket, and I know it isn't true.
Danny Kaye, US entertainer.

Of course it's frightfully dull: that's the whole point.
Line spoken by Robert Morley's character in the film *The Final Test* (1953).

Oh God, if there be cricket in heaven, let there also be rain.
Sir Alec Douglas-Home, British prime minister, from *Prayer of a Cricketer's Wife*.

Cricket is the only game that you can actually put on weight when playing.

Tommy Docherty, Scottish football manager.

Cricket is baseball on valium.

Robin Williams, US comedian, addressing Prince Charles.

I only wish some of the players' trousers fitted better.

The Duke of Edinburgh on the modern game, 1987.

There is nothing wrong with the game that the introduction of golf carts wouldn't fix … It is the only competitive activity of any type, except perhaps baking, in which you can dress in white from head to toe and be as clean at the end of the day as you were at the beginning.

Bill Bryson, *Down Under* (2000).

It's a funny kind of month, October. For the keen cricket fan it's when you realize your wife left you in May.

Denis Norden, quoted in the *Guinness Book of Humorous Sports Quotes* (1996).

OUR GLORIOUS TRADITIONAL ENGLISH GAME

Jeez, it's not even as cold as this in my fridge back in Brisbane.

Jeff Thomson, Australian fast bowler, on the early-season English weather; quoted in Simon Hughes, *A Lot of Hard Yakka* (1997).

Sir – Now I know this country is finished. On Saturday, with Australia playing, I asked a London cabby to take me to Lord's and had to show him the way.

Letter to *The Times*, mid-1970s.

County cricketers have two topics of conversation: 'Me And My Cricket', or, as a high-day-and-holiday equivalent, 'My Cricket And Me'.

Frances Edmonds, 1994.

As a preparation for a Test match, the domestic game is the equivalent of training for the Olympic marathon by taking the dog for a walk.

Martin Johnson in the *Independent*, 1995.

Lunch Feeding frenzy

We used to eat so many salads, there was a danger of contracting myxomatosis.
Former Essex spinner Ray East in A Funny Turn (1983).

Lunchtime saw the same feeding frenzy as at breakfast ... Then, at 4.10 p.m. at most grounds, plates of Hovis suddenly arrived, usually containing processed ham or that funny fish paste out of a jar, along with chocolate mini-rolls, Bakewell tarts and those cakes covered in stringy bits of coconut. The players, led by Gatting, attacked this offering like hyenas, tearing the meat from the bread, and less than sixty seconds later the tea tray was just a mass of discarded crusts and wrappers. You'd never eat this kind of thing in mid-afternoon at home.
Simon Hughes, formerly of Middlesex, describes tea time on the county cricket circuit, in A Lot of Hard Yakka (1997).

Clinching the [County] Championship is a strange sensation … There's more atmosphere in a doctor's waiting room.

Simon Hughes, *A Lot of Hard Yakka* (1997).

He will find that trying to shake up English cricket is like stirring up dead sheep.

Raymond Illingworth, on Lord MacLaurin's appointment as chairman of the England and Wales Cricket Board, 1997.

You should treat women the same way as a Yorkshire batsman used to treat a cricket ball. Don't stroke 'em, don't tickle, just give 'em a ruddy good belt.

Former Yorkshire fast bowler Fred Trueman, quoted in David Hopps, *A Century of Great Cricket Quotes* (1998).

Those who run cricket in this country, especially at the domestic level, are for the most part a self-serving, pusillanimous and self-important bunch of myopic dinosaurs.

Henry Blofeld in the *Independent*.

■ OPIUM-PUSHERS, FAT HAS-BEENS...
and other popular cricketers

Michael Atherton

FEC

Letters allegedly scrawled on the young Atherton's locker at Old Trafford. Cricketing folklore has it that the letters did not, as was commonly assumed, stand for 'Future England Captain', but rather stood for 'F*cking Educated C*nt', the Lancashire players being suspicious of Atherton's Cambridge University background; quoted on cricket365.com.

THE SOILED SKIPPER

Daily Mirror headline after Atherton, then England captain, applied dirt to the ball during a test match against South Africa, 1994.

An earnest young man who probably believes what he reads in the *Guardian*.

Richard Littlejohn, *Daily Mail*, 1996; after meeting Atherton he withdrew this 'monstrous slur'.

Ian Botham

You should have stuck to soccer, lad.

Lords groundsman Len Muncer assesses the early form, early 1970s. Botham also played professional football for Scunthorpe United.

If you've signed the cunt, you can sack the cunt.

Sun editor Kelvin Mackenzie on dispensing with Botham's services as a columnist after he lost the England captaincy, 1981; quoted in David Hopps, *A Century of Great Cricket Quotes* (1998).

This fellow is the most overrated player I have ever seen. He looks too heavy, and the way he's been bowling out here, he wouldn't burst a paper bag.

Harold Larwood, former England fast bowler of 'bodyline' notoriety, speaking in 1983.

To his credit he does not appear to harbour a grudge, despite a pen-portrait I adumbrated for the *Daily Express*, describing him as 'in no way inhibited by a capacity to over-intellectualize'.

Frances Edmonds, in *Another Bloody Tour* (1986).

Botham's idea of team spirit and motivation was to squirt a water pistol at someone and then go and get pissed.

Ray Illingworth advises against Botham's appointment as a 'motivator' for England, 1995.

A drug-crazed opium pusher.

Pakistan bowler Sarfraz Nawaz, as recorded by Botham in *My Autobiography* (1995). Botham was briefly suspended in 1989 for smoking cannabis.

Out! White coats and white sticks: the umpires

What are the butchers for?
US actress Pauline Chase is baffled by the white-coated umpires as she watches her first game of cricket.

Now all you want is a white stick.
Australian batsman Sidney Barnes hands a stray dog to umpire Alex Skelding, during Australia's all-conquering 1948 tour of England. (Skelding had twice given Barnes out lbw.)

The physique of a hat-pin and the only geriatric stoop I have ever seen on a 15-year-old.
Michael Parkinson, another son of Barnsley, recalls his first glimpse of the man who would become Umpire Harold ('Dickie') Bird.

I've lost my marbles.
'Dickie' Bird himself, unable to find his ball counters during a test match, 1996.

Bowden has developed a … repertoire of skittish behaviour which, to some, is hilarious fun but to others is cringe-making and demeaning … For a leg bye, he strokes his thigh in the sort of lascivious manner favoured by comedian Vic Reeves on the game show *Shooting Stars*. The only difference being that Reeves is funny.
John Stern on New Zealand umpire Brent ('Billy') Bowden, March 2004.

The Indians used to call him 'Iron Bottom', but he
wasn't – not after all that fackin' curry.

John Emburey, speaking after Botham's return from a tour of India, quoted in
Simon Hughes, *A Lot of Hard Yakka* (1997).

Geoff Boycott

Next bloody ball, bloody belt it, or I'll wrap your
bat round your bloody head.

Brian Close, comradely advice to his partner during the Gillette Cup final,
1965: quoted by Martin Kelner in the *Guardian*, 8 September 2003.

You have done for Australian cricket what the
Boston Strangler did for door-to-door salesmen.

Telegram from Jack Binney after Boycott took a more than usually long time
to score 50 at Perth, during England's tour of Australia 1978–9.

[Myra] Hindley … only participated in some of the grisliest murders of the 20th century, whereas Geoffrey ran out Derek Randall at Trent Bridge.

Martin Kelner in the *Guardian*, 8 September 2003, referring to the notorious incident in the 1977 Ashes series. Against New Zealand the following year, Ian Botham was sent on with instructions to run Boycott out. 'What have you done? What have you done?' wailed Boycott. Botham's reply was, apparently, 'unprintable'.

To offer Boycott a new contract is akin to awarding Arthur Scargill the Queen's Award to Industry.

Letter to the *Yorkshire Post*, 1984.

The next question has absolutely nothing to do with either music or sport: At which ground did Geoffrey Boycott score his hundredth hundred?

Classic FM, 1992.

The only fellow I've met who fell in love with himself at a young age and has remained faithful ever since.

Dennis Lillee, 1997.

I know why he bought a house by the sea – so he'll be able to go for a walk on the water.

Fellow-Yorkshireman Fred Trueman, on Boycott's move from Yorkshire to Poole, in Dorset, 1997.

Legends Sir Donald Bradman

I've got it – he's yellow!
Reputed comment of England captain Douglas Jardine as
he watched a film of Australia's run-machine Don Bradman
batting at the Oval in 1930. 'It' would turn out to be the
controversial strategy of 'Bodyline' bowling: short-pitched
bowling directed at the batsman's body, primarily intended
to nullify the threat posed by Bradman's prolific scoring
(see Bodyline quotes on page 184–185).

… the Don was too good: he spoilt the game.
A complimentary sort of insult, from England's great
opener Jack Hobbs, 1952.

Mike Brearley

The Ayatollah.

Nickname bestowed on the England captain by Australian barrackers,
1979–80, comparing his beard to that sported by Iran's then spiritual leader,
Ayatollah Khomeini.

Ian Chappell

The godfather of sledging.

Nigel Henderson on the hard-bitten Australian captain of the early 1970s
whose team earned the nickname the 'Ugly Australians', in *The Worst of
Cricket* (2004).

Legends — Denis Compton

One of the most careless runners between the wickets in English cricket history – his batting partners regarded his calls as just a basis for negotiation.
David Hopps in the *Guardian*, 25 May 2004.

Chappell was a coward. He needed a crowd around him before he would say anything. He was sour like milk that had been sitting in the sun for a week.
Ian Botham and Peter Roebuck *It Sort of Clicks* (1986).

Dominic Cork

He's a show pony. He's a prima donna. Cork may have talent but he does have an attitude problem. If you think I was bad, my God, he's three times worse.
Geoffrey Boycott, 1997.

I'm trying to look like Beckham, and it's not working.
Former England bowler Dominic Cork, whose wife is a hairdresser, on his trendy new coiffure, summer 2003.

Black and very blue

Well to be honest, the fackin' facker's fackin' facked.
John Emburey, Middlesex and England off-spinner, reported response to a journalist's enquiry after the state of his injured back; quoted in Simon Hughes, *A Lot of Hard Yakka* (1997).

Colin Cowdrey

**Cowdrey is a big fat fairy,
Fa-la-la-la-la, la, la, la, la.**
The stylish but amply built Kent and England batsman is barracked by Somerset supporters (to the tune 'Deck the Hall with Boughs of Holly') during a one-day game, mid-1970s.

He'll cop it too.
Australian fast bowler Jeff Thomson on the 40-something Cowdrey, summoned to bolster England's batting line-up on England's 1974–5 Ashes tour of Australia, quoted in David Frith, *The Fast Men* (1975).

Graham Dilley

… Dennis Lillee's action with Denis Thatcher's pace.
Geoffrey Boycott on Kent and England fast bowler Graham Dilley, 1982.

Andrew Flintoff

A farmhand delighting in the coconut shy.
Tanya Aldred in *Wisden Cricketers' Almanack* 2004.

Fat Freddie.

Flintoff's nickname in his younger days, quoted in the the *Guardian*,
19 August 2004.

... as uncomplicated as
bangers and mash ...

Mike Selvey in the *Guardian*, 8 September 2003.

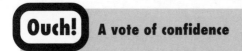

Ouch! A vote of confidence

You know, Fender, there is no man in England whose bowling I would rather face than yours; and there is no batsman in England I would rather bowl against either.

MCC captain Johnny Douglas to all-rounder Percy Fender during the voyage out to Australia for the Ashes series of 1920–1. England lost it 5–0.

Angus Fraser

Eeyore without the *joie de vivre*.

Mike Selvey on the Middlesex and England seamer; in *Wisden Cricketers' Almanack* (1996).

Fraser's approach to the wicket currently resembles someone who has his braces caught in the sightscreen.

Martin Johnson in the *Independent*.

Stephen Fleming

… in turning Test match half-centuries into three figures [Fleming] has a conversion rate equivalent to David Icke's …

Mike Selvey on New Zealand's much-admired captain, in the *Guardian*, 11 June 2004.

Saurav Ganguly

About as warm as a lump of halibut plucked straight from the freezer.

Jim White on India's captain in the *Guardian*, 22 July 2002.

He was a prick, basically, and that's paying him a compliment.

Steve Waugh on the man nicknamed 'Lord Snooty', quoted in Barry Norman 'Cricket Books 2003' in *Wisden Cricketers' Almanack* 2004.

Mike Gatting

Gower: Do you want Gatt a foot wider?
Cowdrey: No. He'd burst.

Exchange between England captain David Gower and bowler Chris Cowdrey, India v. England, Calcutta, 1985.

Hell, Gatt, move out of the way, I can't see the stumps.

Dennis Lillee stops in mid-run-up.

It couldn't have been Gatt. Anything he takes up to his room after nine o'clock, he eats.

Ian Botham on the 'barmaid in the bedroom' affair that cost Gatting the England captaincy in 1988.

Giddo! **Don't let them get up your nose**

Can I have a snort leg for this guy please.
Unidentified Surrey bowler changes the field for new
batsman Ed Giddins, after the latter was banned for two
years by the ECB for testing positive for cocaine, quoted by
Giddins himself, 1996.

If it had been a cheese roll it would never have got
past him.
Graham Gooch on the famous Shane Warne delivery that turned a foot and a
half and clean bowled Gatting, Old Trafford, 1993.

Ashley Giles

Ashley Giles made a simple attempt at a top-edged
hook by Mahela Jayawardene look like a Mr Bean
Christmas special.
Peter Hayter despairs of England's fielding in Colombo in the *Mail on Sunday*,
2003; quoted on www.cricfo.com.

King of Spain.
Nickname for Ashley Giles, 2004, based on a misprint on the mugs created
for his benefit season, which should have read 'king of spin'.

There was a time when a batsman had more chance of being hit by space debris than being done in the flight by Ashley Giles.

Mike Selvey in the *Guardian*, 14 June 2004.

Graham Gooch

If Graham tried harder he could make a successful office boy.

School report.

He is cricket's Thatcher.

The *Sunday Telegraph*, probably intending it as a compliment, 1990.

Darren Gough

You can't have 11 Darren Goughs in your side – it would drive you nuts. It would be like having 11 Phil Tufnells.

England paceman Darren Gough on the future of England's bowling attack; Quotes of the Year, www.telegraph.co.uk, 30 December 2003.

[a] 33-year-old with a dodgy knee, a tendency to pile on the pounds and the promise of a lift to matches by helicopter.

The *Independent's* Stephen Brenkley sees the end of the road in sight for Darren Gough as an international cricketer, spring 2004; quoted on www.cricinfo.org.

David Gower

It's difficult to be more laid back without being actually comatose.

Frances Edmonds in the *Daily Express,* 1985.

He looked so frail and wispish, like a pedigree two-year-old filly, as he walked disconsolately back to his team-mates in the dressing-room.

Frances Edmonds describes Gower's appearance after being dismissed during England's tour of the West Indies, 1986, *Another Bloody Tour* (1986).

Gower is the most disastrous leader since Ethelred the Unready. Beyond question he should now stand down in favour of Ken Dodd.

The *Sun*, after England went 4–0 down against Australia in the 1989 Ashes series.

Tony Greig

There's only one head bigger than Tony Greig's – and that's Birkenhead.

Fred Trueman on the England captain of the mid-1970s.

Steve Harmison

Harmison and Jones sound more like a department store than a pair of fast bowlers.

Anon., spring 2004. Steve Harmison and Simon Jones nonetheless helped England to a 3–0 series victory in the Caribbean.

Legends W.G. Grace

He has one of the dirtiest necks I have kept wicket behind.
Viscount Cobham.

Surely you're not going, Doctor? Why, there's one stump still standing!
Charles Kortwright, Essex fast bowler, to the great man (and well-known non-walker) after unsuccessfully appealing for lbw and a catch, and then demolishing Grace's wicket; quoted by Frank Keating in the Foreword to David Hopps, *A Century of Great Cricket Quotations* (1998).

Unless I'm crackers or something, I've scored a bloody sight more runs than that bearded old bugger.
Geoffrey Boycott on W.G. For the record, Grace scored 55,309 runs in first-class cricket, against Boycott's 56,540.

Graeme Hick

Hick is just a flat-track bully.
Former New Zealand spin bowler John Bracewell on Graeme Hick, during England's 1991–2 tour of New Zealand, quoted in David Hopps, *A Century of Great Cricket Quotes* (1998).

Buttock-clenchingly grim.
Michael Henderson in the *Daily Telegraph*, on yet another test match comeback by Hick, this time against New Zealand in 1999.

At least we are safe from an intoxicated rendition of 'There's only one Graeme Hick'. There are, quite clearly, two of them. The first one turns out for teams like Worcestershire and New Zealand's Northern Districts and plays like a God. The second one pulls on an England cap and plays like the anagram of a god.

Martin Johnson in the *Independent*.

Matthew Hoggard

Shrek.

The Yorkshireman's nickname in the England dressing-room, *c.*2004. A real-life Shrek – Charlie Shreck – plays for Nottinghamshire.

Kim Hughes

[He looked] about as despondent as it would be possible for a man without a noose around his neck to look.

Brian Viner in *The Times*, 2 July 2004, describing the former Australian captain's appearance on television after England came back from the brink of defeat to beat Australia at Headingley in 1981.

Merv Hughes

The mincing run-up resembles someone in high heels and a panty girdle chasing after a bus.

Martin Johnson in the *Independent*, 1993.

A man descended directly from the walrus.

Nigel Henderson describes the moustachioed Australian fast bowling hard-man and champion sledger, *The Worst of Cricket* (2004).

He was so close you could smell his dodgy breath.

New Zealand batsman Mark Greatbatch on being stared down by Hughes, 1993, quoted in Nigel Henderson, *The Worst of Cricket* (2004).

Merv was a hard man to lip-read as his words were delivered through a moustache large enough to house a colony of Koalas, but his lexicon was thought to contain only five words. 'Eff', 'Pommy', 'Yer', 'Off', and 'Bastard'.

Martin Johnson on Merv Hughes the sledger, in the *Daily Telegraph*, 23 July 2004.

Great slow batsmen 1

Johnny-Won't-Hit-Today.
Acronymic nickname of J.W.H.T. Douglas, multi-initialled England captain of the early 1920s, bestowed for his strokelessness.

If there were 22 Trevor Baileys playing in a match, who would ever go and watch it?
Australian opening batsman Arthur Morris on the notoriously slow-scoring England all-rounder of the 1950s; quoted on redscc.org.

You'll never die of a stroke, Mackay.
Fan jeering the slow batting of Ken 'Slasher' Mackay, Australian batsman of the 1950s. The jibe has also been directed at Geoff Boycott by Fred Trueman.

Nasser Hussain

Papadom fingers.
Nickname accorded the Bombay-born Hussain for his habit of sustaining finger injuries.

Now that Nasser's gone, who's going to score the stodgy 32 off 148 balls to shore up the middle order?
'Slogger' in the *Guardian*, 12 July 2004.

In his 96 tests, he has only been run out twice, which draws to mind Jasper's Carrott's joke about his mother-in-law: 'She's been driving for 60 years and has never had an accident – she's seen a few, though.'

David Hopps on Nasser Hussain, after the latter ran out test debutant Andrew Strauss in the first test match between England and New Zealand at Lord's, 24 May 2004, in the *Guardian* 11 May 2004.

Ray Illingworth

If I had my way, I would take him to the Traitor's Gate and personally hang, draw and quarter him.

Ian Botham on the then chairman of the England selectors, 1995.

Inzamam-ul-Haq

Fat potato!

Spectator's shouted comment during a match played in Toronto, Canada. The incensed Inzamam walked into the crowd to confront his abuser.

Robert Key

Bob the Builder.

Nickname for the ample-girthed Kent batsman when he first appeared for England.

Key is a big lad, probably the widest cricketer since Mike Gatting.

Martin Johnson in the *Daily Telegraph*, 26 July 2004.

Brian Lara

Brian, you're turning into a prima donna.

Warwickshire captain Dermot Reeve to Lara, then a Warwickshire batsman, during a match against Northamptonshire, 1995.

Lara apart, no cricketer since Ian Botham has reached the heights and depths of the game quite so spectacularly. When he is good he is sublime … His bad days can veer to the staggeringly inept.

Matthew Engel in the *Guardian*, 2 April 2004. Just 11 days later, at Antigua, Lara had one of his sublime days, scoring 400 not out to break the record for the highest individual test score in the fourth test match against England.

Chris Lewis

We have a gaping hole in the England side because Ian Botham has gone. People say Chris Lewis will take his place and I always say, What, on the bus to the ground?

Fred Trueman on England's under-achieving all-rounder, 1993.

The enigma with no variation.

Vic Marks *in* the *Observer*, 1994.

A cross between a cricketer and a Chippendale.

Nigel Henderson, *The Worst of Cricket* (2004).

The quick stuff

Fast men and not-so-fast men: blood, mums and ... moisturizers

I want to hit you Bailey, I want to hit you over the heart.
South African fast bowler Peter Heine to England's Trevor Bailey, 1950s, recorded by Jim Laker in *Over to Me*.

I enjoy hitting a batsman more than taking him out. It doesn't worry me in the least to see a batsman hurt, rolling around screaming and blood on the pitch.
Alleged remark by Australian fast bowler Jeff Thomson, quoted in David Frith, *The Fast Men* (1975).

I try to hit a batsman in the ribcage when I bowl a purposeful bouncer, and I want it to hurt so much that the batsman doesn't want to face me any more.
Dennis Lillee, quoted in Frith, *The Fast Men* (1975).

The thicker you are, the better your chances of becoming a fast bowler.
Stewart Storey, Surrey coach, 1985.

Fast bowlers are bully boys: They dish it out but they can't take it.
Brian Close, quoted in *Cassell's Sports Quotations* (2000).

On the subject of skin care, James Anderson says: 'I always use a daily moisturiser.' It's one of the great tragedies that Fred Trueman is no longer on Test Match Special, because Jonathan Agnew asking Fred what type of moisturiser he used in his day could have produced one of sport's truly great radio moments.
Martin Johnson, writing in the *Daily Telegraph*, summer 2003.

Corey Collymore and Adam Sanford wouldn't bowl my mum out.
Geoff Boycott, *ad infinitum*, March 2004, on two members of the West Indies much-maligned pace attack in the spring 2004 series against England.

Chris Lewis baldly went where no other cricketer has gone before – and the prat without a hat spent two days in bed with sunstroke.

Vic Marks again, 1994, after a shaven-headed Lewis spent too long in the Caribbean sun.

Dennis Lillee

Are you aware, Sir, that the last time I saw anything like that on a top lip, the whole herd had to be destroyed.

Comedian Eric Morecambe to the handlebar-moustached fast bowler.

Arthur Mailey

I used to bowl tripe, then I wrote it, now I sell it.

Notice above the butcher's shop owned by former Australian leg-spinner and journalist Arthur Mailey.

Devon Malcolm

Who could forget Malcolm Devon?

England committee chairman Ted Dexter forgets fast bowler Devon Malcolm, 1989.

Sometimes it takes him a fortnight to put on his socks.

England team manager Micky Stewart finds Malcolm a little too laid back in the 1990–91 Ashes series.

Telling dear old Devon to bowl down the corridor of uncertainty is like asking bombers to demolish a city without hurting any civilians.

Peter Roebuck in *The Sunday Times*, 1993.

Javed Miandad

As cricketing pains in the arse go, I imagine Javed Miandad takes some beating.

Barry Norman, 'Cricket Books 2003' in *Wisden Cricketers' Almanack*, 2004.

Muttiah Muralitharan

An effing cheat and an effing chucker.

Nasser Hussain's alleged welcome to Muralitharan as he came out to bat at Kandy, second test match between England and Sri Lanka, December 2003, quoted in *Wisden Cricketers' Almanack* 2004. Muralitharan reported the incident to the match referee, but no action was taken. An editorial in a local paper advised Hussain: 'Tread lightly, old boy, tread lightly and mind your manners.'

It makes a joke of the game – it makes me sick talking about it. Everyone knows he bowls illegally. I saw a photo in the paper the other day and put my old school protractor on the arm. It was bent at 48 degrees.

Former Australian wicketkeeper Barry Jarman, quoted in the *Guardian*, 11 May 2004.

A song for Murali

Throw, throw, throw the ball, gently down the seam
Murali, Murali, Murali, Murali, chucks it like a dream
Bowl, bowl, bowl the ball, gently through the air
Murali, Murali, Murali, Murali, here comes Darrell Hair
... No Ball!

England's Barmy Army serenade Muralitharan to the tune of 'Row, Row, Row the Boat'; quoted on www.cricinfo.org. Australian umpire Darrell Hair notoriously no-balled Muralitharan for throwing at Melbourne in 1995.

Future generations will be hoodwinked into believing 'Muchichuckalot' was the best of them all. At best, his action is suspicious. At worst it belongs in a darts tournament.

Chat-show host Michael Parkinson on Muralitharan's controversial action; quoted on www.cricinfo.org.

Dermot Reeve

I don't like you, Reeve. I never have liked you. You get right up my nose and if you come anywhere near me, I'll rearrange yours.

Lancashire coach David Lloyd extends a Big Red Rose Welcome in the Old Trafford committee room, 1995.

Jack Russell

A crackpot behind the stumps as well as being a legendary tea-drinker, recluse, and a man who had steak and chips for 26 consecutive nights on a tour of India.

Tanya Aldred in the *Guardian*, 20 August 2001. Russell pointed out that it was in fact 28 consecutive nights.

Rev. David Sheppard

They say the fool of the family always goes into the Church.

Ted Dexter, after a series of run-outs involving the Sussex and England batsman (and future Anglican bishop of Liverpool) in a match against Australia, 1963.

Graeme Smith

How the fuck are you going to handle Shane Warne when he's bowling into the rough?

Australian opening batsman (and devout Catholic) Matthew Hayden sledges the South African batsman Graeme Smith, playing in his first test series, March 2002, quoted in the *Guardian* 30 October 2002.

David Steele

A bank clerk going to war.

Chris Taylor, the *Sun*, 1976, as the grizzled Northamptonshire and England batsman went out to face the fearsome West Indian pace attack.

Great slow batsmen 2

The programme implied that ... he made love like he played cricket: slowly, methodically, but with the very real possibility that he might stay in all day.

Martin Kelner reviewing a Channel 4 documentary *The Real Geoffrey Boycott*, in the *Guardian*, 8 September 2003.

Watching Tavaré was a bit like waiting to die.

The *Observer Sport Monthly*, on the Kent and England tortoise Chris Tavaré, May 2004.

Only Chris Tavaré could make a sixty-nine boring.

Anon. cricket commentator after Tavaré took almost five hours to score 69 in the first innings of the Ashes test match at Old Trafford in 1981. In the second he took seven hours over 78.

This was batting directed by Ingmar Bergman to a Leonard Cohen soundtrack. A blockumentary. Not quite up there with the absolute masters of the art ... but getting there.

Mike Selvey on New Zealand opening batsman Mark Richardson's 93 in the first innings of the first test match against England at Lord's, 20 May 2004, in the *Guardian*, 21 May 2004.

Graham Thorpe

Thorpy's not the best when he gets hit … he usually has six months out.

Nasser Hussain jokingly questions his friend's hard-man image; quoted on www.cricinfo.com.

Phil Tufnell

The other advantage England have got when Phil Tufnell is bowling is that he isn't fielding.

Former Australian cricketer Ian Chappell on the fifth test, Perth, 1991.

The archetypal fag-puffing, beer-swilling, bird-pulling, bouncer-evading village cricketer who lurked, rather than fielded, in the deep yet somehow made it into the big time.

Barry Norman 'Cricket Books 2003' in *Wisden Cricketers' Almanack* 2004.

Michael Vaughan

Vaughan … still can't toss a salad.

Mike Walters in *The Wisden Cricketer*, June 2004, on England's captain losing his 10th toss in 13 games at Antigua, April 2004.

The captain with a choirboy face and endearing tendency to drop easy catches.

Stephen Moss in the *Guardian*, 19 August 2004.

Shane Warne

You haven't got it, son.

Mike Tamblyn, captain of a Melbourne club side, to the young Shane Warne, quoted in David Foot, *A Century of Great Cricket Quotes* (1998).

Fat boy spin.

Anonymous taunt, punning on musical performer Fat Boy Slim.

Shane Warne's idea of a balanced diet is a cheeseburger in each hand.

Australian wicketkeeper Ian Healy, 1996.

Shooter and zooter, my foot.

Geoffrey Boycott, unconvinced by Warne's new 'mystery ball', in the *Sun*, 1994.

Poisoned by his mother? It is good, very good. It ranks up there with 'I got it from the toilet seat.'

Dick Pound, chairman of the World Anti-Doping Agency, on Warne's explanation that he tested positive for a banned substance because he had taken a diuretic given to him by his mother; Quotes of the Year, www.telegraph.co.uk, 30 December 2003.

Steve Waugh

Australian cricket's Mr Gradgrind.

David Hopps in the *Guardian*, 7 July 2001.

... Steve Waugh spent the whole series giving out verbals – a bit of a joke when he was the one bloke wetting himself against the quick bowlers.

England captain Mike Atherton, 1994.

Oy Stephen, best batsman in the world? You ain't even the best batsman in your family!

Member of the Barmy Army barracks Steve Waugh; quoted by Nasser Hussain in 'Trying to Melt the Iceman', in *Wisden Cricketers' Almanack* 2004.

With the possible exception of Rolf Harris, no other Australian has inflicted more pain and grief on Englishmen since Don Bradman.

Mike Walters in the *Mirror*, on Steve Waugh's retirement.

Bob Willis

A 1914 biplane tied up with elastic bands trying vainly to take off.

Frank Keating on England's fast bowler of the 1970s and early 1980s, in the *Guardian*.

■ THE TEST-PLAYING NATIONS
a short guided tour

Cricket-playing nations are only capable of limited amounts of sexual activity.

Letter to the *Bangkok Post*, 1991.

Australia

See pages 184–192.

Bangladesh

… no-hopers who would struggle to cut the mustard in Minor Counties cricket.

The *Mirror*'s Mike Walters, after England's test victories over Bangladesh, 2003.

England

The usual permutation of plebs: a few Gentlemen, some Professionals, a couple you'd rather not introduce to your mother – and at least one you'd cross Oxford Street to avoid.

Frances Edmond on the England team of the 1980s; in the *Daily Express*.

Men against boys.

BBC TV commentator sums up the West Indies' 5–0 'blackwash' of England in 1984.

England have only three major problems: they can't bat, they can't bowl, and they can't field.

Martin Johnson in the *Independent*, as England began their 1986–7 tour of Australia. England proceeded to win the series 2–1, the last time they defeated Australia in a series.

CLOGGED!

Sun headline after an England team was defeated in Holland, 1989.

BOMBAY POTATOES

Sun headline after England were defeated by India, 1993.

A LOAD OF LANKAS!

Sun headline after England were defeated by Sri Lanka, 1993.

When the pressure point comes, English cricketers crumble.

Shane Warne, 1997.

Champion whingers of the world.

Former Indian opening batsman Sunil Gavaskar on England, January 2002.

India

A dry fart!

England spinner Philippe Edmonds's reply on being asked what he most looked forward to on returning to England from a tour of India.

I just want to get into the middle and get the right sort of runs.

England batsman Robin Smith during a diarrhoea-blighted tour of India, 1993.

I've done the elephant. I've done the poverty. I'd might as well go home.

Phil Tufnell nears the end of a tour of India, 1993.

New Zealand

Like batting against the World XI at one end and Ilford Second XI at the other.

Mike Gatting on the respective strengths of Richard Hadlee and the other New Zealand bowlers, 1986.

Pakistan

Pakistan is the sort of place every man should send his mother-in-law to, for a month, all expenses paid.

Ian Botham, 1984.

Someone get this buffoon out of here.

England captain Mike Atherton gets bored with the faltering English of Pakistani Press Association's Asghar Ali, at Rawalpindi during the 1996 World Cup.

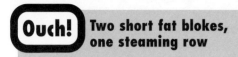
Fucking cheating cunt.

Pakistani umpire Shakoor Rana to England captain Mike
Gatting, Faisalabad, 1987. Rana became angry when
Gatting moved a fielder, and Gatting responded in kind.
The test match was suspended until Gatting was persuaded
to give Rana a handwritten apology.

I think he is not the son of man. That is why his face is from a white monkey.

Gatting described in a letter to Rana from the Depot Chief
of Lahore Railways, 1987.

South Africa

You guys are history.

England fast bowler Devon Malcolm reacts to being struck on the helmet by South African bowler Fanie de Villiers, 20 August 1994. Stung, Malcolm went on to take 9 South African wickets for 57 runs at the Oval.

Zimbabwe

We murdered them … We flippin' hammered them.

England coach David Lloyd, nicknamed 'Bumble', rants and raves as England fail by one run to defeat Zimbabwe in the first test, Bulawayo, 1996.

West Indies

If the West Indies are on top, they are magnificent. If they are down, they grovel … I intend to make them grovel.

Perhaps the rashest words in test cricket history, spoken by South African born England captain Tony Greig, 1976. Rampant in batting and bowling, West Indies won the ensuing test series 3–0, not just ramming Greig's intemperate prediction down his throat, but also ushering in 20-odd years of West Indian fast-bowling dominance.

West Indies minus Ambrose = Poms

Banner at an Australia v. West Indies test match, Perth 1997, alluding to the already declining West Indies. But Curtley Ambrose still managed to bowl the West Indies to victory on this occasion.

This team cannot bat through 90 overs because they can barely sit through a feature film … the young players probably think the Three Ws was a restaurant.

B.C. Pires on the West Indies' batting frailties, in the *Guardian*, spring 2004. (The Three Ws are Weekes, Worrell and Walcott, legendary West Indian batsmen of the 1950s.)

I'm not going to write off Bangladesh. The way we're playing at the moment you can't write off anybody at all.

Wetst Indian captain Brian Lara, quoted in the *Wisden Cricketer*, June 2004.

I am not saying the players will get any better – but they can't become any worse.

Former West Indies fast bowler Colin Croft on the West Indies side of 2004; quoted on www.cricinfo.org.

[There is] only one thing more to be said, with apologies to Norwegian football commentator Borg Lillelien: Lord Learie Constantine! Sir Garry Sobers! Sir Vivian Richards! Bob Marley! The Jamaican Olympic bobsleigh team! Sir Trevor McDonald – can you hear me, Sir Trevor McDonald? Your boys took one hell of a beating!

Peter Hayter, adapting Borg Lillelien's famous words (see page 108), celebrates England's 3–0 defeat of the West Indies, spring 2004 (their first series victory in the Caribbean since 1967–8), quoted on www.cricinfo.org.

■ THE ASHES
120 years of injury and insult

In affectionate remembrance of English cricket, which died at the Oval on 29th August, 1882. Deeply lamented by a large circle of sorrowing friends and acquaintances. RIP. NB The body will be cremated and the ashes taken to Australia.

Anonymous notice in the *Sporting Times*, 2 September 1882, after England's defeat by Australia that year. The 'body' was the set of stumps used in the match, which were ceremonially burned and put in an urn; the origin of the name 'The Ashes'.

If we don't beat you, we'll knock your bloody heads off.

England fast bowler Bill Voce to Australia's Viv Richardson at the opening of the infamous 'Bodyline' series of 1932–3.

All Australians are an uneducated and unruly mob.

England captain Douglas Jardine to Australian wicketkeeper 'Stork' Hendry, during the acrimonious 1932–3 series. England tour manager Sir Pelham ('Plum') Warner later said of Jardine: 'He is a queer fellow. When he sees a cricket ground with an Australian on it, he goes mad.'

I don't want to speak with you, Mr Warner. Of two teams out there, one is playing cricket, the other is making no effort to play the game of cricket.

Australian captain W.M. Woodfull's comment to England's team manager 'Plum' Warner when the latter called on the Australian dressing-room after the Australian captain had been hit over the heart by a ball from the England fast bowler Harold Larwood, during the 'Bodyline' tour, January 1933.

Bodyline bowling … is causing intensely bitter feelings between the players as well as injury. In our opinion it is unsportsmanlike. Unless stopped at once, it is likely to upset the friendly relations between Australia and England.

Telegram from the Australian Cricket Board to the MCC. The MMC 'deplored' the complaint and denied any fault on the part of England's bowlers, 1933. Bodyline tactics were seldom used after 1933.

I have on occasions taken a quite reasonable dislike to Australians.

Former England captain Ted Dexter, 1972.

No good hitting me there mate, nothing to damage.

England batsman Derek Randall to Dennis Lillee after the fast bowler had hit him on the head with a bouncer, Melbourne 1977.

Lillee and Thomson

Ashes to ashes, dust to dust

G'day, howya going?
Australian fast bowler Dennis Lillee greets Queen Elizabeth II,
Lord's 1972.

**I couldn't wait to have a crack at 'em [England].
I thought: 'Stuff that stiff upper lip crap. Let's see
how stiff it is when it's split.'**
Australian fast bowler Jeff Thomson in *Thommo Declares*
(1986).

**Ashes to ashes, dust to dust
If Thomson don't get ya, Lillee must.**
Caption to a cartoon in the *Sydney Telegraph*, 1975,
referring to Dennis Lillee and Jeff Thomson, fearsome
destroyers of England's batting in the 1974–5 Ashes series.

At least I have an identity. You're just Frances Edmonds's husband.

Australian wicket-keeper Tim Zoehrer to England left-arm spinner (and
husband of Frances) Philippe Edmonds, 1980s; quoted in the *Guardian*
30 October 2002.

A fart competing with thunder.

England captain Graham Gooch on England's attempts to beat Australia in
the 1990–91 Ashes series.

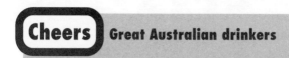

Cheers Great Australian drinkers

Yeah, I'd drink with 'em. Trouble is, you can never find any Poms to drink with, can you Dennis?
Jeff Thomson offers the Poms a tinnie, 1974–5.

In my day, 58 beers between London and Sydney would have virtually classified you as a teetotaller.
Ian Chappell on Australian batsman David Boon's record-breaking consumption of 58 cans of beer on the flight to England for the 1989 Ashes tour.

It must stand for 'Overwhelmingly Beaten Englishman'.
Ian Chadband, when Graham Gooch was awarded an OBE shortly after England had lost the 1994–5 Ashes series.

I am not talking to anyone in the British media – they are all pricks.
Australian captain Allan Border, 1993.

The traditional dress code of the Australian cricketer is the baggy green cap on the head and the chip on the shoulder. Both are ritualistically observed.
Simon Barnes in *The Times*.

... a makeshift outfit that couldn't win an
argument with a drover's dog.

Jeff Thomson on England's bowling attack during the 1997 Ashes series.

Q: What is the height of optimism?
A: An English batsman applying sunblock.

Q: What do you call an Englishman with 100
   runs against his name?
A: A Test bowler.

Disparaging Australian riddles doing the rounds during Australia's successful
2001 tour of England.

CRASH, BANG, WALLABY

Sun headline on Monday 9 July 2001, after a weekend that saw Australian
teams defeat the Lions at rugby union and England at cricket and
Australian tennis player Pat Rafter reach the Wimbledon men's final in
which he met Goran Ivanisevic (who had defeated Britain's perennial
Wimbledon hopeful, Tim Henman, in the Wimbledon men's semi-final).

ENGLAND FALL TO WINDOW CLEANER

Headline of a report in the *Guardian* 25 October 2002 by Stephen Bishop.
Callum Thorp, a window cleaner, took 4 for 58 as England made 221 on the
first day of their opening tour match against Western Australia at Perth.

Australia could happily swap Steve and Mark for their younger brothers Dean and Danny – and throw mum Bev and dad Rodger in the IX – and still horsewhip England within three days.

Chris Ryan on the possibility of dropping the Waugh twins for the 2002–03 Ashes series in Australia. 'England can't even tie their own shoelaces', in the *Guardian* 25 October 2002.

These tourists seem a pale imitation of the bulldog brigade seen in previous decades. They must prove they belong to the tradition of Ken Barrington and Herbert Sutcliffe or else this must be the last time their country is invited to play a five-match series, a custom that insults other countries and flatters their own.

Harsh words from the *The Age* (Melbourne), 8 November 2002, as England suffer a disastrous first day in the first test match at Brisbane. Australia ended the day at 364 for 2, with Matthew Hayden 186 not out.

Playing in the early 1970s, England were the team to beat. I hardly think 30 years later we can put them on the same footing as New Zealand.

Former Australian leg-spinner Kerry O'Keeffe after England lost the first Ashes test of the 2002–03 series by a massive margin; quoted in the *Guardian*, 13 November 2002.

Barracking
A great Australian art form

Don't give the bastard a drink – let him die of thirst.
Advice from the Australian crowd, directed at the England captain Douglas Jardine during the 1932–3 'bodyline' series.

Leave our flies alone, Jardine … They're the only friends you've got in Australia.
More advice to Jardine from the same, 1932–3.

Bailey, I wish you were a statue and I was a pigeon.
Barracker from Sydney's famous 'Hill', 1950s, taunts the slow-scoring Englishman Trevor 'Barnacle' Bailey.

I didn't know they stacked crap that high.
Australian crowd member barracks the 6 ft 5 in England fast bowler Bob Willis during the 1970–1 Ashes tour down under.

Come on, Brearley! You make Denness look like Don Bradman.
Crowd member to England's cerebral captain, during the Melbourne test match, 1978–9 (Mike Denness was England captain in the 1974–5 Ashes series when Denness – and England – were cut to pieces by Dennis Lillee and Jeff Thomson).

GOLD MEDALLION AWARD FOR GREATEST WHINGER WOULD HAVE TO BE WON BY J.M. BREARLEY, CLASSICAL MUSIC LOVER
The ultimate insult. Banner waved at Melbourne, England v. Australia, 1979–80.

That Randall! He bats like an octopus with piles.
Australian cricket fan on England's Derek Randall during
the 1982–83 England tour of Australia; quoted in *Wisden's
Cricketer's Almanack*, 1994.

Tufnell, can I borrow your brain. I'm building an idiot.
Australian barracker to Phil Tufnell, 1994–5.

Count 'em yourself, you Pommie c***.
Even their umpires do it ... Australian umpire Peter
McConnell to Phil Tufnell when the England spinner asked
how many balls were left in the over, second test match of
the 1990–91 series, quoted in Nigel Henderson *The Worst of
Cricket* (2004).

ENGLAND WILL WIN IF CAMILLA PARKER BOWLS
Australian fans' banner, 1995.

John Howard, Sir Donald Bradman, Banjo Patterson, Rolf Harris, Richie Benaud, Dawn Fraser, Malcom Conn, Kerry Packer, Dame Edna Everidge, your boys took one hell of a beating.

Another ironic echo of the famous commentary of the Norwegian Borg Lillelien (see pages 108 and 183). Mike Selvey on England's consolation victory on the fifth test of the 2002–03 Ashes series; in the *Guardian*, 7 January 2003.

There are three great international team sports in Australia: cricket, rugby (two codes), and Pom-bashing. But the greatest of these is the last, and it is time we prepared ourselves for the greatest celebration of Pom-bashing since Bodyline, the 1930s cricket tour that became an international incident. That one rankles to this day and is otherwise known as the longest whinge in sporting history.

Simon Barnes in *The Times*, writing before the rugby World Cup final, November 2003.

When I say you'll lose the Ashes 3–0 I mean it as a compliment.

Australian fast bowler Glenn McGrath on his prediction for the 2005 Ashes series in the light of resurgent England's successful performances against New Zealand and the West Indies in 2004. 'You guys shouldn't be too upset with that,' McGrath went on. 'You should treat it as praise. Before every other series I reckoned we were going to beat you 5–0.' Quoted in the *Independent*, 7 August 2004.

■ FOUR-EYED FUCKERS AND UNFIT FAT TWATS
a short history of sledging

Don't get him out just yet, Johnny, he smells so bloody lovely.

Yorkshire wicketkeeper Don Brennan to spin bowler, Johnny Wardle, Yorkshire v. Oxford University; quoted in David Hopps, *A Century of Great Cricket Quotes* (1998).

Bad luck, sir – you were just getting settled in.

Yorkshire's Fred Trueman to a Varsity batsman, bowled first ball after much protracted wicket-prodding; quoted in David Hopps, *A Century of Great Cricket Quotes*.

Don't bother shutting it, son, you won't be out there long enough.

England bowler Fred Trueman as a new Australian batsman closed the gate on his way out of the pavilion at Lord's, early 1960s.

Hey Garth, look at this four-eyed fucker. He can't fucking bat, knock those fucking glasses off him straight away.

Australian captain Bobby Simpson to bowler Garth MacKenzie, Trent Bridge, 1964, on the entry of a bespectacled Geoffrey Boycott.

Who's this, then? Father fucking Christmas?

Australian fast bowler Jeff Thompson on the arrival at the crease of England's silver-haired and bespectacled David Steele, Lords, 1975. In the event, 'Father fucking Christmas' did rather well.

Just remember one thing son, you've already been killed once on the cricket field.

Ian Botham to New Zealand's Ewen Chatfield after the latter had run out Derek Randall while backing up in a test match at Christchurch, 1977–8. (Two years earlier Chatfield's heart had stopped beating for several seconds after he was hit on the temple by a bouncer from England's Peter Lever.)

What do you think this is, a fucking tea party? No, you can't have a fucking glass of water. You can fucking wait like the rest of us.

Allan Border to Robin Smith, Trent Bridge, 1989.

You've got to bat on this in a minute, Tufnell. Hospital food suit you?

Australian fast bowler Craig McDermott, parting words after being dismissed by Phil Tufnell, 1991.

Tickets, please!

Javed Miandad, having just dismissed Merv Hughes. Hughes had earlier called the Pakistan bowler 'a fat bus conductor'.

I'll bowl you a fucking piano, yer Pommie poofta, let's see if you can play that.

Merv Hughes to an unnamed English batsman.

Go and deflate yourself, you balloon.

South African batsman Daryll Cullinan to Australia's Shane Warne during a
one-day international at Sydney, 1997.

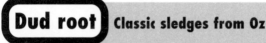 Classic sledges from Oz

How's your wife and my kids?
An old favourite, first recorded as being from Rodney
Marsh to Ian Botham.

Your missus is a dud root, mate.
From any Australian wicketkeeper.

Back to the nets, dickhead.
From any Australian wicketkeeper.

Better ease off a bit, this one's still on the tit.
Captain to fast bowler on entry of young(ish) batsman.

**Q: What's the difference between a Pom and a bucket
of shit?**
A: The bucket, mate.
Australia v. England, anytime, anywhere.

There's two pieces of shit together.
On a mid-wicket batsmen's conference.

We've got him four floors up, now take him to the sixth.
Captain to fast bowler, indicating a bouncer is required.

You've just dropped the World Cup, mate.

Australian captain Steve Waugh to Herschelle Gibbs, who had just dropped the Australian captain in the 1999 World Cup final. Gibbs had been throwing the ball up to celebrate. Waugh went on to score a century, and Australia won by two runs.

You don't get a runner for being an overweight, unfit, fat twat.

Australian wicketkeeper Ian Healy to Sri Lanka's Arjuna Ranatunga, who had asked for a runner as he had 'sprained something' during the humidity-affected WSC cup final at Sydney. Healy's riposte was broadcast around the ground through the effects microphone.

Around the wicket, umpire, and call an ambulance.

Yorkshire fast bowler Steve Kirby, as Lancashire batsman Chris Schofield arrived at the wicket.

Let's get Alec Bedser out.

Glamorgan captain Robert Croft to his teammaes as veteran fast bowler Martin Bicknell of Surrey comes out to bat in a National League match on 14 September 2003, quoted on www.cricinfo.com.

■ SLEDGE AND COUNTER-SLEDGE
the all-time top 10

It's red, round, and weighs about five ounces.
  Glamorgan bowler Greg Thomas to Somerset batsman
  Viv Richards, who had just missed two deliveries, 1986.

You know what it looks like, now go and fetch it.
  Viv Richards to Greg Thomas, having just hammered the
  next delivery out of the ground.

**Don't you be staring at me, man! Get back and bowl.
This is my island. This is my culture. You have no right
to be staring.**
  Viv Richards takes guard against Australia's Merv Hughes,
  West Indies tour match.

In my culture we say 'Piss off'.
  Hughes to Richards, having bowled him with the fifth ball.

  Umpire to Leicestershire medium-pacer Gordon Parsons,
  who has bowled a bouncer that Viv Richards has hit out of
  the ground:
That's your one bouncer for the over, Gordon.

  Viv Richards, on one knee, to the umpire:
**No, no umpire, hey man please, he can bowl as many of
those as he wants!**
  Quoted by Piers Morgan in the *Observer Sports Monthly*,
  5 September 2004.

You can't fucking bat.

Merv Hughes to Robin Smith after beating him outside the off stump, 1989.

Hey Merv, we make a fine pair: I can't fucking bat and you can't fucking bowl.

Robin Smith to Merv Hughes, having driven the next ball for four. Smith went on to make a century.

Warne: I've been waiting for two years to have another bowl at you.

Cullinan: Looks like you spent most of it eating.

Exchange between Shane Warne (Australia) and Daryll Cullinan (South Africa), reported by Simon Hughes in *Yakking Round the World* (2000).

McGrath: Why are you so fucking fat?

Brandes: Because every time I fuck your wife she gives me a biscuit.

Glenn McGrath (Australia, thin) and Eddo Brandes (Zimbabwe, not thin), recorded in the *Guardian*, 30 October 2002. The Australian slip fielders were, apparently, helpless with mirth.

Allan Donald, bowling short to Allan Lamb:

Lambie, if you want to drive, go hire a car.

Allan Lamb, having cover-driven the next ball for four.

Go park that one.

Exchange during a county championship game between Warwickshire and Northamptonshire.

McGrath: What's Lara like in bed, mate?

Sarwan: Why don't you ask your wife?

Glenn McGrath walks into another ambush, this time by West
Indies vice-captain Ramnaresh Sarwan, fourth test match,
Antigua, 2003. Amazingly, McGrath complained about
Sarwan's riposte to umpire David Shepherd; Sarwan scored a
match-winning 105 and McGrath finished on 1/50. From
www.crikey.com.au.

**Arjuna, he's probably slotting himself around at 150 kilos at
the moment, is he? Swallowed a sheep or something like that.**

Shane Warne on the rotund Sri Lankan Arjuna Ranatunga;
quoted on 'Quotes of the Week', bbc.co.uk, February 2004.

**It is better to swallow a sheep or a goat than swallow
what he has been swallowing.**

Ranatunga's response. Warne was banned from cricket for a
year for testing positive for a banned diuretic.

**Flintoff to Smith: Come on lads, let's get Ed out so that he
can go beagling on the Downs.**

Smith to Flintoff: You don't know what beagling is.

**Flintoff to Smith: OK, let's get him out so that he can go
punting on the Cam.**

Exchange between Lancashire's Andrew Flintoff and Kent's
Cambridge-educated Ed Smith, summer 2003, recorded in
Ed Smith's diary of the 2003 season.

■ FROM THE COMMENTARY BOX

The umpire signals a bye with the air of a weary stork.
John Arlott, BBC radio commentary.

He approaches the wicket like Groucho Marx chasing a pretty waitress.
John Arlott, describing an unidentified player's bowling action. From a BBC radio commentary.

He didn't quite manage to get his leg over.
Jonathan Agnew, BBC Radio commentator, referring to an incident in which batsman Ian Botham accidentally collided with his own wicket after turning suddenly and failing to step over the bails. Agnew's gaffe caused fellow-commentator Brian Johnston to collapse in helpless laughter, one of radio sport's most cherished moments.

This is Cunis at the Vauxhall End. Cunis – a funny sort of name. Neither one thing nor the other.
Alan Gibson, cricket commentator, analyses the name of the New Zealand medium-pacer, 1969.

This bowler's like my dog: three short legs and balls that swing both ways.
Brian Johnston.

Cakes and bails — Legends of the commentary box

He sounds like Uncle Tom Cobbleigh talking to the Indians.
Dylan Thomas on John Arlott, letter, 11 July 1947.

He has the watchfulness of a gentlemanly salamander.
Steve Jacobi on Richie Benaud in the *Observer Sports Monthly*, May 2004.

[He eyes] the lens with the manner of a disdainful lizard.
Brian Viner on Richie Benaud in *The Times*, 2 July 2004.

Johnston's enduring contribution to Western civilization is the cake-by-cake commentary.
The Times, obituary of Brian Johnston, 1994.

Born with a diamond-encrusted golden spoon thrust well down the throat.
Don Mosey, sportswriter, *The Alderman's Tale* (1991), on Christopher Martin-Jenkins, BBC radio cricket commentator.

There is a lounge-lizard narcissism about this fellow that brings to mind the Yiddish phrase that translates to: 'Of all his mother's children, he loves himself to death.'
Matthew Norman on Channel 4 cricket's Mark Nicholas; 'Mr Smug's bails must be removed', in the *Evening Standard*, 24 May 2004. Norman also described Nicholas as '… simpering to camera in the self-besotted manner of one who's been told he has bedroom eyes.'

You've come over at a very appropriate time. Ray Illingworth has just relieved himself at the pavilion end.

Brian Johnston welcomes TV viewers to Grace Road, Leicester, 1970s.

The bowler's Holding, the batsman's Willey.

Brian Johnston, 1976.

Batsmen wear so much protection these days that I generally identify them from their posteriors.

Brian Johnston uses binoculars during the 1988 Benson and Hedges Cup final.

We didn't have any metaphors in my day. We didn't beat about the bush.

Fred Trueman, 1995.

Turner looks a bit shaky and unsteady, but I think he's going to bat on – one ball left.

Brian Johnston, as New Zealand batsman Glenn Turner was struck in the box area, with one ball of the over remaining.

Australia 602 for 6 dec., England 20 for 3. And in the fifth Test, victory is possibly slipping away from England.

Steve Rider, BBC TV.

Rugby Union

Ruck 'n' Roll

Rugby is a good occasion for keeping thirty bullies far from the centre of the city.
Oscar Wilde.

A game played by fewer than fifteen a side, at least half of whom should be totally unfit.
Michael Green, *The Art of Coarse Rugby* (1975).

Rugby is a game for the mentally deficient...
That's why it was invented by the British. Who else but an Englishman could invent an oval ball?
Peter Pook *Pook's Love Nest.*

A bomb under the West car park at Twickenham on an international day would end fascism in England for a generation.
Philip Toynbee.

Grandmother or tails, sir?
Anon. rugby referee to Princess Anne's son Peter Phillips, Gordonstoun School's rugby captain, for his pre-match coin-toss preference.

Men do not greet one another like this ... except perhaps at rugby club dinners.
Alan Cooper, defence counsel, whose client had been accused of having unlawful sexual congress with a dolphin, 1991.

League or Union?

Anyone who doesn't watch rugby league is not a real person. He's a cow's hoof, an ethnic, or comes from Melbourne.

John Singleton, *Australian*, 1981.

I'm 49, I've had a brain haemorrhage and a triple bypass and I could still go out and play a decent game of rugby union. But I wouldn't last 30 seconds in rugby league.

Graham Lowe, 1995.

If union is the game they play in heaven, then God, please send me to hell.

Letter to the *Daily Telegraph* from a rugby league fan less than impressed with the 2003 Rugby (Union) World Cup; quoted on bbc.co.uk, October 2003.

I think you enjoy [rugby] more if you don't know the rules. Anyway, you're on the same wavelength as the referees.

Jonathan Davies, *A Question of Sport*, BBC TV, 1995.

If the game is run properly as a professional game, you do not need 57 old farts running rugby.

Will Carling on the English Rugby Football Union, 1995.

■ RUGGER BUGGERS
players and coaches

Neil Back

Get off, you look ugly.

Australian referee Peter Marshall to blood-spattered England flanker Neil Back after he complained about being ordered to the blood bin in England's World Cup match against South Africa, November 2003.

Bill Beaumont

Blimey, there's a bird just run on the park with your arse on her chest.

Steve Smith to England captain Bill Beaumont as a topless, 40-inch-chested Erica Roe appears on the pitch at Twickenham, 1982.

In the scrum — Cauliflower ears

> … lumpy, misshapen ears … are an occupational hazard among players who spend a lifetime with their heads between other men's legs in the scrum.
>
> The *Guardian*, 3 October 2003.

David Campese

How rich is that? This coming from a bloke who could be passed off as a turnstile. I think I've already made more tackles in one season of rugby than he did in his entire career. The bloke should go live in Holland and make his living as a windmill … I wonder about Campo. How does he live with himself? How does it feel to be a man with no friends in rugby?

Australian international Wendell Sailor on his compatriot David Campese, who had criticized Sailor's ability to tackle the opposition, in the *Sun-Herald*, (Australia), 22 September 2002.

Will Carling

He runs like a castrated calf.

Australian winger David Campese on former Engand centre and captain Will Carling.

Forwards and backs

Mothers keep their photo on the mantelpiece to stop the kids going too near the fire.
Jim Neilly, BBC TV, 1995, on the Munster pack.

Traditionally, forwards are very fat and drink huge quantities of beer (or, in the case of former England 'prop' Colin Smart, aftershave), and backs are willowy, sylph-like and probably studied classics at Peterhouse, Cambridge. But times have changed: in the professional era … everyone has gone fitness crazy, and backs and forwards all now look the same: fit, bronzed, 17 stone, with rectangular heads.
The *Guardian*, 3 October 2003.

Rugby backs can be identified because they generally have clean jerseys and identifiable partings in their hair … Come the revolution, the backs will be the first to be lined up against the wall and shot for living parasitically off the work of others.
Peter Fitzsimmons, quoted on rugbyforum.co.za.

The Holy Writ of Gloucester Rugby Club demands: first, that the forwards shall win the ball; second, that the forwards shall keep the ball; and third, the backs shall buy the beer.
Doug Ibbotson.

The scrum is essentially a boxing match without the Queensberry rules: it is home to punching, gouging and testicle twisting.
The *Guardian*, 3 October 2003.

A word sign beginning with the letter P was the signal for the forwards to go right. When, predictably, Gareth Edwards called 'psychology' half the forwards went left.
Carwyn James on an outbreak of 'signals ambiguity' in the Welsh pack.

Lawrence Dallaglio

He's been a prat.

Clive Woodward on Lawrence Dallaglio after the latter allowed himself to become the victim of a Sunday newspaper 'sting' in May 1999.

Christophe Dominici

He is an imbecile.

French rugby coach Bernard Laporte on French wing Christophe Dominici, who dropped the ball as he went to touch down for an easy try in France's Six Nations game against Italy, 21 February 2004; quoted in the *Guardian* 23 February 2004.

Bob Hiller

Bob Hiller had the hair of a city slicker and the hoofing toecap of a Tunisian mule.

Frank Keating on the England fullback of the 1970s.

Martin Johnson

A tall glowering dour bugger.

Colin Meads, New Zealand rugby legend (and something of a tall glowering dour bugger himself), on England's 6 ft 7 in World-Cup-winning rugby captain; quoted in the *Evening Standard* 18 November 2003.

Johnson's neck may be turning into export-quality timber.

Anon., 2004.

Plop it over How to kick a penalty

… my kicking style … is inspired by sitting on the toilet.

Mark Woodrow, whose six penalty goals helped Pertemps Bees (aka Birmingham-Solihull) eject Wasps from the Powergen Cup; quoted in the *Evening Standard*, 1 March 2004.

Jason Leonard

You have to prove you're not just a crafty cockney accumulating caps.

England coach Jack Rowell to Jason Leonard, 1990s. Prop forward Leonard had the last laugh, outlasting Rowell and accumulating caps under his successor Clive Woodward, and eventually winning a World Cup winner's medal in 2003.

Trevor Leota

At his worst, he could not hit a cow's behind with a banjo …

Chris Hewett on Wasps' huge Samoan hooker; in the *Independent* 1 June 2004.

Jonah Lomu

There's no doubt about it, he's a big bastard.

Gavin Hastings, 1995.

He's a freak and the sooner he goes away the better.

England captain Will Carling licks his wounds after a rampaging Lomu had almost single-handedly crushed England in the World Cup semi-final, Cape Town, 18 June 1995.

Colin Meads

Colin Meads is the kind of player you expect to see emerging from a ruck with the remains of a jockstrap between his teeth.

Tony O'Reilly on the legendary All Black lock forward (nicknamed 'Pine Tree'), quoted in the *Guinness Book of Humorous Sports Quotes* (1996).

He liked to bite the heads off terrified opponents and spit them between the posts.

The *Guardian*, 3 October 2003.

Brian Moore

I think Brian Moore's gnashers are the kind you get from a DIY shop and hammer in yourself. He is the only player we have who looks like a French forward.

Paul Rendall on the England hooker of the 1990s, quoted on rugbyforum.co.za.

The scrum-half

Scrum-half: a small, irritating man with thinning hair who shouts a lot.

The *Guardian*, 3 October 2003.

Dean Richards

Dean Richards is nicknamed Warren, as in warren ugly bastard.

Jason Leonard on the legendary Leicester and England No. 8, 1995.

Jack Rowell

… Rowell, an immensely successful businessman, has the acerbic wit of Dorothy Parker and, according to most New Zealanders, a similar knowledge of rugby.

Mark Reason *Total Sport*, 1996, on England's coach for the 1995 World Cup, the year they were destroyed by New Zealand's Jonah Lomu.

Dorian West

What sort of name is Dorian for a rugby player? I just hope, for his sake, that he isn't selected against Australia, New Zealand or South Africa. And if he plays alongside fellow England front-row man Julian White, surely all will be lost. Stick to croquet, guys.

The *Guardian* on the England and Leicester prop forward, 3 October 2004.

Jonny Wilkinson

Many people are bored to death by Jonny … If it was meant to be a kicking game William Webb Ellis would never have picked up the ball and ran with it in the first place – that was the idea.

Former New Zealand winger Grant Batty on Jonny Wilkinson, quoted in the *Guardian*, 18 November 2003.

Sweet young boy's face on Schwarzenegger bone structure.

Natasha Joffe on Jonny Wilkinson, 'Jonny Come Lately' in the Guardian 25 November 2003.

A boring, self-centred prat.

A Brisbane newspaper columnist on Jonny Wilkinson before England's World Cup final victory, November 2003. Not just libellous, but almost certainly blasphemous as well.

… come on, what is it with the hands? Are they cupped in prayer, Jonny? Or fear? Do they signify membership of a secret society?

Jonny Wilkinson's cupped hands are declared the most irritating trait in sport, *Observer Sport Monthly*, May 2004.

Keith Wood

Uncle Fester.

Nickname for the bald Irish hooker for his supposed resemblance to the *Addams Family* character.

Sir Clive Woodward

Chairman of the Bored.

The *Herald Sun,* Sydney on England's coach, 19 November 2003.

The Black Knight.

Nickname applied to Woodward in Australia, 2004.

His success and the knighthood have inflated his ego beyond the size of the new Wembley Stadium if he truly believes that he will be a viable successor to Eriksson by 2006.

Matt Dickinson in *The Times*, 1 September 2004, after reports linking Woodwood with a move into football management.

■ THE WORLD IN DISUNION
international rugby

Australia

The females and children are fine and seem to be perfectly normal human beings but what are we going to do with this thing called the Australian male?

England and Leicester utility back Austin Healey on Australians, during the 2001 Lions tour of Australia; quoted in the *Guardian*, 20 November 2003.

England

The English are fat and useless.

Free-running French fullback Serge Blanco, *c.*1990.

Of all the teams in the world you don't want to lose to, England's top of the list. The English know no humility in victory or defeat … If you beat them, it's because you cheat. If they beat you, it's because they've overcome your cheating. Good teams learn how to win and lose with graciousness and humility. England hasn't learned that lesson yet.

Grant Fox, New Zeland fly-half, 1993, quoted on rugbyforum.co.za.

Wales v. England

Trust and understanding

Look what these bastards have done to Wales. They've taken our coal, our water, our steel. They buy our houses and they only live in them for a fortnight every twelve months. What have they given us? Absolutely nothing. We've been exploited, raped, controlled and punished by the English – and that's who you are playing this afternoon.

Phil Bennett psychs his lads up for Wales v. England, 1977.

Like you, we came under the yoke of our Anglo-Saxon brothers. You, wisely though, had much more sense than us in that you devoured as many of them as you could.

Alan Thomas, Welsh Rugby Union president, welcomes the Fijians in 1985.

The relationship between the Welsh and the English is based on trust and understanding. They don't trust us and we don't understand them.

Dudley Wood, 1986.

The biggest sell-out since Gallipoli.

Dick McGruther, chairman of the Australian RFU, on England's sending a weak and inexperienced squad to Australia in 1998 on what became known as 'the tour from hell'. A team that included Jonny Wilkinson lost a test match 76–0.

England boring? We're talking about a nation whose idea of risk-taking is to buy a ticket in the pools. Whose idea of excitement is to join a queue. This is a country where the liveliest sporting action is to be found under the staircase at Buckingham Palace.

Australian journalist Mike Gibson in the *Daily Telegraph*, November 2003.

Thugby White orcs on steroids

When they ran on to the field, it was like watching a tribe of white orcs on steroids. Forget their hardness – has there ever been an uglier forward pack? ...

Michael Laws, New Zealand sports columnist, on the England pack; in 'Quotes of the Year', sport.telegraph.co.uk, 30 December 2003.

He'll probably stamp on your head and go for your kidneys.

Anon. Australian on what to expect from an England player if you meet one, June 2004, quoted by Robert Kitson in the *Guardian*, 22 June 2004.

WORLD CHAMPIONS OF THUGBY

Headline in an Australian newspaper following England's controversial and disastrous tour of New Zealand, summer 2004.

The English are so arrogant. That's why they went to war in red uniforms. There is this cockiness about them that rubs us up the wrong way.

Australian back-row forward Toutai Kefu in the *Herald Sun*, 19 November 2003. The article in question was headlined 'Why We Hate Them All'.

F is for France and flair – the two words go together as naturally as 'England' and 'mechanical'.

The *Guardian* 3 October 2003.

The only memories I have of England and the English are unpleasant ones. They are so chauvinistic and arrogant.

French back-row forward Imanol Harinordoquy destroys any lingering vestiges of entente cordiale …

You either like or you don't like the English. Most people hate them. Personally I don't have much love.

French coach Bernard Laporte stokes up the war of words ahead of the rugby World Cup semi-final with England, Monday, 10 November, 2003, quoted on bbc.co.uk.

France

Playing the French is like facing 15 Eric Cantonas: they are brilliant but brutal.

England hooker Brian Moore, 1995.

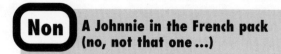

Non A Johnnie in the French pack (no, not that one ...)

PLAY SAFE, PASS IT TO CONDOM
Banner waved during an international match during the 1980s, when the French side included a lock forward by the name of Jean Condom.

CONDOM IS BACK IN FRENCH PACK
Headline in the *Independent*, 1980s.

A Frenchman went to the lavatory, he was in there
   quite a while.
A Frenchman went to the lavatory, he was do-ing
   it in style.
Whe-en su-dden-ly there aro-ose, a cry of anguish
   – and despair,
'OÙ EST ... LE PAPIER ...? OÙ EST ... LE
   PAPIER ...?'

The Marseillaise is given a new lease of life by English rugby fans at Twickenham, 2000s.

Ireland

They think we're just a bunch of ignorant paddies
from the bog. Let's not disappoint them.

Irish player Stewart McKinney before a test match against England, quoted on rugbyforum.co.za.

Italy

Woodward labelled the Italians dangerous, but he was probably referring to their driving rather than their rugby.

Martin Johnson (sports journalist) in the *Daily Telegraph* 16 February 2004. Referring to Woodward's comments before England's Six Nations game against Italy on 14 February.

New Zealand

New Zealanders are tough as teak, densely muscled and bear-like – and that's just the players' wives.

The *Guardian* 3 October 2003.

World chumps.

New Zealand's *Sunday Star-Times* newspaper on New Zealand's defeat to Australia in the rugby World Cup semi-final, November 2003.

Running rugby Kiwi-style ...

Andrew Mehrtens loves it when Daryl Gibson comes inside of him.
Anon. New Zealand commentator.

Scotland

If you can't take a punch, you should play table tennis.

French coach Pierre Berbizier after accusations of foul play after a France v. Scotland Five Nations match, 1995.

The French pulled up the Scots' kilts and discovered they had no balls.

Former New Zealand forward Zinzan Brooke on Scotland's 51–9 defeat by France in the 2003 World Cup; quoted in sport.telegraph.co.uk, 30 December 2003.

Wales

No leadership, no ideas. Not even enough imagination to thump someone in the line-out when the ref wasn't looking.

JPR Williams, after a 28–9 defeat by Australia in 1984.

We've lost seven of our last eight games. The only team we've beaten is Western Samoa. It's a good job we weren't playing the whole of Samoa.

Gareth Davies, 1989.

■ THAT LITTLE TRIP DOWN UNDER
November 2003

IS THAT ALL YOU'VE GOT?

Headline in *The Australian* above a photo of Jonny Wilkinson during the
2003 Rugby World Cup, after Wilkinson's kicking had helped England to
victory in their group game against South Africa.

THANKS POMS
FOR SENDING
MY ANCESTORS
TO
AUSTRALIA!
YOU BEAUTY!

Poster in an Australian rugby fan's car parked outside the England rugby
team's hotel, November 2003.

What's with the Poms whingeing about the
Wallabies whingeing? They do more whingeing
about our whingeing than what we actually whinge.

A whingeing letter to the *Sydney Morning Herald*, November 2003.

HANDS UP IF YOU THINK WE'RE BORING

Back-page headline in the *Sydney Daily Telegraph* above a photograph of
England's rugby players with their arms raised to applaud their World Cup
semi-final victory against France, November 2003. The headline beneath ran
'Wallaby greats say dull England are killing rugby.'

DANGER – BORING RUGBY TEAM TRAINS HERE

Sign on Sydney's Manly Beach near England's hotel, quoted on bbc.co.uk.

In the pouring rain, the wretched English hung us out to dry.

French newspaper *Le Parisien*, after France's 7–24 defeat by England in a rain-sodden World Cup semi-final, 15 November 2003.

English rain, English game, English penalties and thus English victory.

French newspaper *Le Monde* after the same; 15 November 2003. England's coach, Clive Woodward, when asked if the wet conditions had favoured England, responded, 'It rains in France as well, you know.'

Rain, shine or hail, the Six Nations Disease will influence the outcome of Saturday's World Cup final. Undoubtedly, like myxamatosis, botulism, swine fever and foot-and-mouth, it is here to stay.

Sydney Morning Herald columnist castigates England's style of play, November 2003.

That's not rugby! That's just gutless shit!

'Rampaging' Roy Slaven in an Australian TV 'satire', on England's 24–7 defeat of France in the World Cup semi-final, quoted in the *Guardian*, 20 November 2003.

England 20 Australia 17

READ IT AND WEEP

Headline in the Sydney *Sun-Herald*, 23 November 2003, after Jonny Wilkinson's last-minute drop goal won the World Cup for England.

JONNY ROTTEN

Headline in the Sydney *Sunday Telegraph*, 23 November 2003.

There are a lot of you Brits about. At least the weather's nice for you. That will be some comfort when you lose.

'Man on the Sydney harbour ferry', on the forthcoming Rugby World Cup Final, quoted in *The Guardian*, 20 November 2003.

IF YOU WANT TO XXXX THE AUSSIES, USE A JONNY

England supporters' banner at the Rugby World Cup final, Sydney, November 2003. The rest is history.

After The *Sun* had urged its readers to bombard the Australian High Commission in London until the 'missing' ball with which Jonny Wilkinson kicked England to World Cup glory was returned to England:

Want the ball? Then give us the Ashes.

Sydney *Daily Telegraph*, 6 December 2003.

Postscript — England's sweet chariot in the ditch

The crown is askew, and suspicions are growing in the southern hemisphere that the crown may even be a fake.

Stephen Jones in *The Sunday Times*, 13 June 2004, after England's 36–3, post-World Cup defeat by the All-Blacks at Dunedin's 'house of pain'.

Sir Clive Woodward's sweet chariot [has] lurched into the ditch.

Hugh McIlvanney in *The Sunday Times*, 13 June 2004, after the same defeat.

They may have the William Webb Ellis Trophy but they never beat New Zealand getting it and they never would have.

Dale Budge, 20 June 2004 on tvnz.co.uk, after England's post-World Cup 2–0 series loss to the All Blacks, June 2004.

Any lingering respect for England's achievement at the World Cup has disappeared quicker than a dingo's lunch.

Robert Kitson in the *Guardian*, 22 June 2004, as England arrive in Australia to play a test match, June 2004. England were trounced 51–15, their fifth loss in eight games since their victory in the World Cup final.

Tennis

Gayest of Sports

Tennis doesn't encourage any kind of intellectual development. The dumber you are on court, the better you're going to play.

Jim Courier, 1999.

Tennis now looks more like a computer game than a sport. Played not by people but by sponsored humanoids …

Bryan Appleyard in *The Sunday Times*, 6 June 2004.

Tennis is, probably in all senses of the word, the gayest sport …

Will Buckley in the *Observer*, 27 June 2004.

■ TENNIS PLAYERS
a load of wankers

Tennis players are a load of wankers. I'd love to put John McEnroe in the centre for Fulham [Rugby League Club] and let some of the big players sort him out.

Colin Welland, playwright, 1980.

André Agassi

André Agassi was recently born again. Now, if he can only grow up…

Sports Illustrated, 1990.

Looks like he missed the last train to Woodstock. With neon-coloured spandex worn under denim-look shorts, he's tennis's flower-child gone to seed.

Mr Blackwell, *Tennis*, on the young Agassi, 1990.

Moby with a tennis racket.

The *Guardian* on a less hirsute Agassi, *c.*2004; 'Wimbledon 2004: The Definitive Guide'.

Boris Becker

An endearingly hideous paradigm of pubescent gaucheness.

Matthew Norman remembers the 17-year-old Boris Becker who won Wimbledon in 1985, in a review of Becker's ghosted autobiography, *Evening Standard*, 7 June 2004. Norman went on: 'Unseeded then, all too seeded later, alas, in the Nobu broom cupboard' (see box).

Never having met Becker, I can't comment on whether he is, indeed, a motherf***** or even an arsehole, but, having read this book, I can safely say that 'Becker', the fairy-tale hero, is a jerk.

Bryan Appleyard, reviewing Becker's autobiography for *The Sunday Times*, 6 June 2004. Appleyard seems particularly riled by the fact that 'Becker loves the worst kind of bad, bloke pop'.

Knobbing at Nobu

'Five minutes of small talk, then into the nearest suitable corner for our business.' Right little charmer, eh?

Bryan Appleyard quotes from and comments on Becker's account in his autobiography of the notorious 'sex in the cupboard' episode at London's Nobu restaurant, in *The Sunday Times*, 6 June 2004.

A ginger Moses called on to lead his people out of the post-war bondage of guilt towards the promised land of international acceptance.

Matthew Norman in the *Evening Standard*, 7 June 2004.

Bjorn Borg

Like a Volvo, Bjorn Borg is rugged, has good after-sales service, and is very dull.

Clive James on the five-times Wimbledon winner of the 1970s, in the *Observer*, 29 June 1980.

Bjorn Borg looks like a hunchbacked, jut-bottomed version of Lizabeth Scott, impersonating a bearded Apache princess.

Clive James compares the Superswede to a blonde bombshell movie star of the 1940s.

Jennifer Capriati

[Resurrected] from oblivion, where she picked up Mike Tyson's body.

Matthew Norman in the *Evening Standard* Supplement: 'Wimbledon 2004', June 2004, referring to Capriati's teenage drug problems, from which she bounced back after rehabilitation.

Lindsey Davenport

The Dumptruck.

Nickname for the American player in her younger, plumper days.

Winning or losing, she has the demeanour of a bored teenager who's been dragged off Tomb Raider to kiss a mad auntie with whiskers.

The *Guardian* on 'the tour's head girl', 17 June 2004.

Chris Evert

Taut and tight-lipped mistress of the baseline … Evert is the all-American golden girl become the champion of monotony.

Paul West, quoted in the *Guinness Book of Humorous Sports Quotes* (1996).

Roger Federer

His only weakness is heavy metal music.

Andrew Castle on the man nicknamed the 'Fed Express', BBC TV, 29 June 2004.

ROGER BLUBBERER

Part of a headline in the *Daily Mail*, 5 July 2004 after a sobbing Federer had won his second Wimbledon title. After winning his first Wimbldeon title in 2003 Federer had also sobbed his heart out and was later given a cow, named Juliet, by a grateful Swiss nation.

Vitas Gerulaitis

Everyone thinks my name is Jerry Laitis and they call me Mr Laitis. What can you do when you have a name that sounds like a disease?

Gerulaitis himself, 1977.

Sebastian Grosjean

Rivals Gordon Kay in his portrayal of a stereotypical Frenchman. It's all there: the air of nonchalance, the unkempt long brown hair ... Could not be any more French if he propped up a bike and started selling Gaultier kilts.

The *Guardian* 'Wimbledon 2004: The Definitive Guide'.

Daniela Hantuchova

Only thermal imaging cameras were able to detect her presence on court.

The *Guardian*, 17 June 2004; on the then extremely svelte Slovakian at Wimbledon in 2003.

Ivan Lendl

I was thrilled until I learned Ivan Lendl had finished above me.

Footballer Ally McCoist, 1990, quoted in the *Guinness Book of Humorous Sports Quotes* (1996). A comment made after he (McCoist) was voted the fifth best-looking sportsman in the world.

Ivan Lendl is a robot, a solitary, mechanical man who lives with his dogs behind towering walls at his estate in Connecticut. A man who so badly wants to have a more human image that he's having surgery to remove the bolts from his neck.

Tony Kornheiser in the *Washington Post*.

Tim Henman

See 'Tiger' Tim, pages 247–250.

Lleyton Hewitt

The constant plucking of his racket strings makes him look like a shuffling madman playing a tiny magic harp that only he can hear.

The *Guardian* 'Wimbledon 2004: The Definitive Guide'.

... that cocky young ocker.

Matthew Norman on Hewitt at Wimbledon, in the *Evening Standard* 'Wimbledon 2004', June 2004.

Billie-Jean King

You'll be good, because you're ugly, Billie Jean.

Frank Brennan, US sportswriter.

Big noises — In women's tennis

Grunter extraordinaire.
The *Evening Standard* on the high-volume Yugoslav Monica Seles, whose grunts reached a level of 93.2 decibels in 1993.

The Queen of Screams.
Nickname of the teenage Russian Maria Sharapova, *c.*2004. According to the *Evening Standard*. Sharapova's grunts reached a level of 86.3 decibels during the 2004 Wimbledon quarter-finals: 'the same as standing beside a high-revving motorcycle, or the screech of a gibbon in the zoo'.

Deafening champion.
The *Evening Standard* on Serena Williams at Wimbledon 2004, defending her 2003 title. Williams's on-courts grunts were recorded at 77.6 decibels.

Anna Kournikova

It's bad enough to enough to default in the first round, but it's the worst thing to default to Kournikova.
Lindsay Davenport on a distressing side-effect of injury.

We all like each other except Kournikova, no-one likes her.
Patty Schnyder speaks for the players on the women's circuit.

Anna's TV gig makes her tennis look good.

The *New York Post* on the non-achieving player's brief and farcical stint as a reporter for the cable channel USA Network, 1 September 2003.

I'm not the next Anna Kournikova. I want to win matches.

The beautiful teenager Russian Maria Sharapova denies any similarity with the beautiful Russian former teenager Anna Kournikova; quoted in the *Guardian*, 17 June 2004.

Svetlana Kuznetsova

Legs of which Mark Hughes would be proud.

The *Guardian* 'Wimbledon 2004: The Definitive Guide'.

John McEnroe

Super Brat.

McEnroe's nickname, bestowed for the British tabloids for his on-court tantrums, 1979.

John McEnroe has hair like badly turned broccoli.

Clive James in the *Observer*, 1980s.

I don't know that my behaviour has improved that much with age. They just found someone worse.

Jimmy Connors, on losing his bad-brat image to John McEnroe, 1984.

McEnroe was as charming as always, which means that he was as charming as a dead mouse in a loaf of bread.

Clive James in the *Observer*, 1980, after John McEnroe had won that's year's Benson and Hedges Cup.

[Federer is] an immeasurably more charming human being than McEnroe (then again, so was Pol Pot).

Matthew Norman in the *Evening Standard*, 21 June 2004.

Amélie Mauresmo

France's Tim Henman, only with bigger shoulders.

The *Guardian* 'Wimbledon 2004: The Definitive Guide'.

One of the few women even more Amazonian than [Jennifer Capriati].

Brian Viner in *The Times*, 2 July 2004.

Ilie Nastase

Nastase is a Hamlet who wants to play a clown, but he is no good at it…

Clive James, the *Observer*.

The best of Super Brat

Man, you cannot be serious!

McEnroe to Wimbledon judge Edward James when the latter called a serve deep that had thrown up a spray of chalk, during a first-round march with Tom Gullikson, 1981; quoted in John McEnroe, *Serious* (2002).

You guys are the absolute pits of the world, you know that?

McEnroe to Wimbledon judge Edward James after another disputed point in the same match. James, believing that McEnroe had called him 'the *piss* of the world', awarded a point against McEnroe.

We're not going to have a point taken away because this guy is an incompetent fool.

McEnroe, having called out the Wimbledon referee in protest at the above, points at Judge James.

You're a disgrace to mankind!

McEnroe to Wimbledon judge George Grime after an 'out' call in McEnroe's semi-final with Australian Rod Frawley.

You can't see as well as these fucking flowers – and they're fucking plastic.

To a Wimbledon line judge, 1981.

What other problems do you have besides being unemployed, a moron and a dork?

To a spectator.

You got a fucking appointment to get to? What the fuck do you care, asshole?

To a fan who objected to him holding up play by challenging a call.

You effing son of an effing bitch. I'm going to effing do you and, if you report me, I'll effing do you again.

To centre court judge Reg Lord, 2 July 1991, as remembered by Lord himself in an interview in the *Guardian*, 17 June 2004.

Look, Nastase, we used to have a famous cricket match in this country called Gentlemen versus Players. The Gentlemen were put down on the scorecard as 'Mr' because they were gentlemen. By no stretch of the imagination can anybody call you a gentleman.

Trader Horn, British tennis umpire.

I feel like dog trainer who teach dog manners and graces and just when you think dog knows how should act with nice qualities, dog make big puddle and all is wasted.

Ion Tiriac, on being Nastase's trainer, 1972.

When Ilie Nastase's winning he's objectionable. When he's losing, he's highly objectionable.

Adrian Clark.

Martina Navratilova

The chubby Plain Jane from the Eastern Bloc ...

Martin Johnson in the *Daily Telegraph*, 22 June 2004, on the young Navratilova, 1973 vintage.

A surly, chunky, rude and mildly paranoidova whom we knew, for ease, as Miss Navrat.

Matthew Norman in the *Evening Standard*, 5 July 2004.

Sure I know where the press room is – I just look for where they throw the dog meat.
Martina Navratilova, 1983.

It's difficult to play against a man ... I mean against Martina.
Navratilova's fellow Czech, Hana Mandlikova, 1984.

Mark Philippoussis

... the knees of an arthritic 93-year-old.
Matthew Norman on Philippoussis at Wimbledon, in the *Evening Standard* Supplement, 'Wimbledon 2004', June 2004.

 The Poo kicks up a stink

Warning, Philippoussis.
Umpire Enric Molina to Mark Philippoussis after a foul-mouthed outburst during his match against Tim Henman at Wimbledon, 2004.

I should give you a warning because you suck.
Philippoussis' reply, quoted on bbc.co.uk.

Once he was the Scud. Then he was the Poo.

Kevin Mitchell on the Australian's changing nicknames, in the *Observer*, 27 June 2004.

Andy Roddick

For almost three sets, Roger Federer played his absolute worst, while Andy Roddick, the world's second-best player, played very nearly his best... and there was next to nothing to choose between them.

Matthew Norman in the *Evening Standard*, 5 July 2004.

Greg Rusedski

I get a kick out of hearing him pick up the accent. He's using words such as 'brilliant' and 'lovely'.

André Agassi, 1995, after the Canadian Rusedski had decided to represent Britain.

If Rusedski was taking performance-enhancing drugs, they obviously didn't work.

Posted on the internet by just about everybody in 2003, when the Canadian was being investigated for an alleged doping offence.

If February 9 is to be the date Greg Rusedski's career ends, he will have crashed out of the game the way he played his tennis — whining, wailing and making excuses.

The *Mirror*. Rusedski was in fact cleared and went on playing.

Marat Safin

… the most unstable temperament since Henry VIII.

The *Guardian* 'Wimbledon 2004: The Definitive Guide'.

A riddle wrapped inside an enigma surrounded by a lunatic.

The *Guardian* on the 'mad monk', 17 June 2004, echoing Winston Churchill's famous description of Russia.

More temperamental than a pre-glasnost submarine.

Evening Standard Supplement: 'Wimbledon 2004', June 2004.

Pete Sampras

Pete the chimp.

Nickname bestowed for the seven-times Wimbledon champion's supposedly simian qualities.

Sampras may the greatest male tennis player ever, but … he is also one of the dullest human beings.

Matthew Norman in the *Evening Standard*, 5 July 2004.

Maria Sharapova

Kourniclona.

HBO reporter to the then 13-year-old blonde Russian, who responded: 'No thank you. I want to be a winner'.

The women's game

From frilly knickers to Amazonians

I don't play if lady umpires. I go to movies and have
a few beers.

Ilie Nastase on umpire Natalie Cohen, 1976.

At Wimbledon, the ladies are simply the candles on the cake.

John Newcombe.

I may have exaggerated a bit when I said that 80 per cent of the top women tennis players are fat pigs. It's only 75 per cent.

Richard Krajicek, 1992.

I'll put Billie-Jean and all the other Women's Libbers back where they belong – in the kitchen and the bedroom.

Bobby Riggs, US tennis player, in 1973, after challenging the Wimbledon women's champion to a singles match. Billie-Jean King won.

Women's tennis is two sets of rubbish that lasts only half an hour.

Pat Cash.

A wading pool has more depth than women's tennis.

The Australian newspaper laments the state of women's tennis in Australia; on tennis-x.com.

... most women players look like Martin Johnson these days.

The *Guardian* 'Wimbledon 2004: The Definitive Guide'.

... she is very nearly as pretty as [Wayne] Rooney.

Simon Barnes on the 2004 Wimbledon ladies champion, in *The Times*, 2 July 2004.

Venus and Serena Williams

An orange crochet hussy dress modelled after something that Wilma Flintstone might choose ... the stylistic equivalent of trash talk.

Washington Post fashion writer Robin Givhan, on Serena's latest outfit.

The All England Club ... would have pitched him [Henman] in the women's event were it not for the fear he might meet a Williams sister and have his spine snapped.

Martin Samuel, *The Times*, July 2002.

■ COME ON, 'TIGER' TIM!

If Tim Henman wins Wimbledon, I am going to do this show in one of Sue Barker's old dresses.

Pat Cash, 1987 Wimbledon champion and BBC commentator, makes a pledge.

The word 'dull' appears to creep into people's conversations whenever Henman's name comes up.

Saj Chowdhury, *BBC Sport Online*, 6 July 2001.

WIMPLEDON CHAMPION

Headline in *The Times*, July 2002.

[Henman] might as well be playing a game of croquet for all the fire he exudes. He's about as sexy as a venetian blind.

Stefanie Marsh in *The Times*, July 2002.

Can there ever have been a 'sports personality' more lacking in wit, charm, imagination and style than Tim Henman?

Bryan Appleyard in *The Sunday Times*, 6 June 2004.

Aah **Mummy's little soldier**

He is such a mummy's boy, only a large number of tattoos could save him.
Neil Stevenson, editor, *The Face*.

This year ... Henman is trying his very best to get tough. He's grunting and growling and returning serve with the kind of filthy looks he hasn't had cause to throw since his wild teenage years when he threw a strop over not being allowed to watch Pogle's Wood and he had to be sent to bed without any tea.
Aidan Smith in the *Scotsman*, 3 July 2002.

Tim is Friends! Tim is a film where someone dies young from cancer. Tim is a chick thing ... Mummy's Little Soldier ...
Martin Samuel in *The Times*, July 2002.

Henman wears his hair short and neat in a manner that demanded the quip: 'Well, his mammy turns him out awfie nice.'
Aidan Smith in the *Scotsman*, 3 July 2002.

If he was any more wholesome you could take him for constipation.
The *Guardian* 'Wimbledon 2004: The Definitive Guide'.

Stop Pumping that fist!

His fist-pumping is manufactured and insincere, like a boy in a playground.
in *The Times*, July 2002.

... he scampers back to the baseline pumping his fist, not like a natural-born winner intent on closing out the match, but like some bored school-kid playing scissors, paper, stone.
Tim Henman's fist is declared the second most irritating trait in sport, in the *Observer Sports Monthly*, May 2004.

Tim Henman is going to be a father again: so that means at least one British seed got through ...

Lenny Henry *The Lenny Henry Show*, BBC TV, 11 June 2004.

He can make a five-set melodrama out of any three-set stroll.

Simon Barnes in *The Times*, 18 June 2004.

The Beatification of the Divine Loser of All England.

Matthew Norman on Henman at Wimbledon, in the *Evening Standard* 'Wimbledon 2004', June 2004.

The timid Tiger who makes even a gentle walk in the park seems like an intrepid venture into the jungle.

Matt Hughes in the *Evening Standard*, 23 June 2004.

■ WIMBLEDON
68 years of hurt (and counting)

Ten of the world's greatest rareties:
No. 4: a British player with a can of silver polish.
'Journolists', column in the *Mail on Sunday*.

A traditional fixture at Wimbledon is the way the
BBC TV commentary box fills up with British
players eliminated in the early rounds.
Clive James, the *Observer*, 1981.

Wimbledon fortnight … the most boring sporting
event on Earth. Two weeks of wall-to-wall tedium,
the only excitement coming when they pull the
covers over when rain stops play.
Edward Richards, *Sydney Morning Herald*, 9 July 2003.

… things traditionally English, such as
strawberries and cream, Cliff Richard and
queuing, and a resignation to the fact that the
overseas player will always triumph.
The Keith Prowse ticket agency website, 2004.

Silencing Sir Cliff – for ever

[a retractable centre court roof] could also mean that Sir Cliff Richard will never again be allowed to 'entertain' the Centre Court crowd during a rain break. Although a tennis fan and a regular attendee at SW19, Richard is believed to have been called into action on Centre Court just the once. It is an indication of how traumatic his brief appearance was that many people think it is an annual occurrence.

Eve Fodens, *The Scotsman*, 6 January 2004, on the advantages of the retractable Centre Court roof, planned for 2006.

It must be a comedy if a British player is winning at Wimbledon!

Serena Williams looks forward to *Wimbledon*, a film which depicts a plucky Briton coming from nowhere to win the tournament. bbc.co.uk, 8 June 2004.

Will Henman Hill become Parmar's Pimple?

David Mellor speculates on Britain's tennis future after Henman (Arvind Parmar, then ranked Britain's No. 2, was ranked 162nd in the world in July 2004), in the *Evening Standard*, 2 July 2004.

It is about as majestic as a broom cupboard, and more likely to contain Barbara than Charles Windsor.

Harry Pearson on the royal box in the *Guardian* 'Wimbledon 2004: The Definitive Guide'.

The French Open

Gallic poncery of the worst kind

Nothing in global sport is so metronomically mind-numbling as tennis on the Paris clay ... I urge you to watch the French Open as God intended, on Ceefax.

Matthew Norman on the French Open, *Evening Standard*, 24 May 2004.

Even now, there are black polo neck-clad men in the bars of the Left Bank, discussing the French Open as if it was some new proposition from Jacques Derrida. For me, the simple act of watching two people chop the ball back and forth with those insane girly spins, then whacking their soles to dislodge the clay, feels like Gallic poncery of the worst kind.

Matthew Norman again.

The US Open Nuremberg, NY

The crowds at Flushing Meadow are about as impartial as a Nuremberg Rally.
Ian Wooldridge in the *Daily Mail*, 1995.

… ladies are asked not to wear hats, as these might prevent Kevin Keegan and Emma Thompson getting a full view of the British women's No 1 being eliminated in straight sets by a pimply teenager from Tajikistan.
Harry Pearson on the royal box again.

Golf

Too Boring (even) for Canada

According to locker-room lore, the name 'golf' arose by default – all the other four-letter words had already been taken.

George Pepper, quoted in the *Guinness Book of Humorous Sports Quotes* (1996).

Golf is too slow a game for Canada. We would go to sleep over it.

John B. McLenan, 1891.

Golf is an ineffectual attempt to direct an uncontrollable sphere into an inaccessible hole with instruments ill-adapted to the purpose.

Sir Winston Churchill.

Golf is a game to be played between cricket and death.

Colin Ingleby-McKenzie, cricketer.

I don't want to play golf. When I hit a ball, I want someone else to go chase it.

Rogers Hornsby.

Golf is a game that needlessly prolongs the lives of some of our most useless citizens.

Bob Hope.

TV golf

If you want to take long walks, take long walks. If you want to hit things with sticks, hit things with sticks. But there's no excuse for combining the two and putting the results on television. Golf is not so much a sport as an insult to lawns.
National Lampoon, 1979.

There is one thing in this world that is dumber than playing golf. That is watching someone else play golf. What do you actually get to see? Thirty-seven guys in polyester slacks squinting at the sun. Doesn't that set your blood racing?
Peter Andrews.

I'd rather watch a cabbage grow than a man worrying his guts over a two-foot putt.
Michael Parkinson (a former president of the Anti-Golf League).

If I had my way, any man guilty of golf would be barred from any public office in the United States and the families of the breed would be shipped off to the white slave corrals of Argentina.
H. L. Mencken.

Writers against golf!

Golf is a good walk spoiled.
Mark Twain.

I regard golf as an expensive way of playing marbles.
G.K. Chesterton.

It's not in support of cricket, but as an earnest protest against golf.
Max Beerbohm, subscribing a shilling to the W. G. Grace testimonial fund.

The uglier a man's legs are the better he plays golf. It's almost a law.
H. G. Wells, *Bealby* (1915).

A golf course outside a big town serves an excellent purpose in that it segregates, as though a concentration camp, all the idle and idiot well-to-do.
Osbert Sitwell.

Golf is typical capitalist lunacy.
George Bernard Shaw.

He enjoys that perfect peace, that peace beyond all human understanding, that peace which cometh at its maximum only to a man who has given up golf.
P.G. Wodehouse.

I have never been depressed enough to take up the game.
Will Rogers.

If I had my way the social status of professional golfers would be one notch below that of Nazi war criminals.
Andy Lyons in *Melody Maker*, 1988.

Golf is like an 18-year-old girl with the big boobs. You know it's wrong but you can't keep away from her.
Val Doonican, Irish singer and entertainer.

Golf and masturbation have at least one thing in common. Both are a lot more satisfying to do than they are to watch.
'Anon', the well-known pseudonym of Onan.

Golf combines two favourite American pastimes: taking long walks and hitting things with sticks.
P.J. O'Rourke.

■ THE GOLFERS
men in ugly pants, walking ...

Ian Baker-Finch

Ian Baker-Flinch.

Perhaps the cruellest nickname ever coined in golf. After winning the 1991 Open, the Australian Baker-Finch's game crumbled; quoted in 'The champion who fell to pieces' in the *Guardian* 13 July 2004.

Billy Casper

I have a furniture problem: my chest has fallen into my drawers.

Casper on himself.

It takes a lot of guts to play this game, and by looking at Billy Casper you can tell he certainly has a lot of guts.

Gary Player.

John Daly

A mullet par excellence, big, blonde and deeply unfashionable ... an all-American mission statement that said 'I'm from Arkansas and I don't give a shit.'

Gavin Newston on the hairstyle of the man known as 'Wild Thing'; in *John Daly: the Biography* (2003).

Wear it if it clashes ...

Golf is a game where white men can dress up as black pimps and get away with it.
Robin Williams, US comedian, 1986.

Golf is not a sport. Golf is men in ugly pants, walking.
Robin Williams, 1986.

No golfer ever swung too slow. No golfer ever played too fast. No golfer ever dressed too plainly.
Rosie O'Donnell.

'Play It As It Lies' is one of the fundamental dictates of golf. The other one is 'Wear It If It Clashes'.
Henry Beard, *Golfing*, 1994.

Doug Sanders' outfit has been described as looking like the aftermath of a direct hit on a pizza factory.
Dave Marr, 1983.

I was distracted by Jesper Parnevik's outfit. I simply couldn't believe the colour of his trousers.
Mark Roe after being disqualified from the Open for signing the wrong scorecard; Quotes of the Year, www.telegraph.co.uk, 30 December 2003.

Fore! Beware of the chief!

Gerald Ford – the most dangerous driver since Ben-Hur – has made golf a contact sport. There are 42 golf courses in the Palm Springs area and nobody knows which one Gerald Ford is playing until after he has teed off. It's not hard to find Gerald Ford on a golf course – just follow the wounded.
Bob Hope.

I would like to deny all allegations by Bob Hope that during my last game of golf, I hit an eagle, a birdie, an elk and a moose.
Gerald Ford, 38th US president.

Whenever I play with him, I usually try to make it a foursome – Ford, me, a paramedic, and a faith healer.
Bob Hope.

When Bill Clinton played golf … he wore jogging shoes, and his shirt was hanging out over painter's pants. Golf needs Clinton like it needs a case of ringworm.
Rick Reilly in *Sports Illustrated*, 1992.

A demon-infested, two-bottles-a-night Caliban of the fairways, with far more interest in destroying himself than any golf course.
Matthew Norman in the *Evening Standard*, 19 July 2004.

David Duval

The strangest man in golf… he went from challenging Tiger Woods to falling off the earth.

Marino Parascenzo in the *Guardian*, 18 June 2004.

Nick Faldo

The only time he opens his mouth is to change feet.

Golfer and TV commentator David Feherty, on Faldo.

I would like to thank the press from the heart of my bottom.

Nick Faldo after winning the Open in 1992.

David Feherty

I keep thinking that I might go out and play like Jack Nicklaus, but instead it's more like Jacques Tati.

David Feherty, 1992.

I was swinging like a toilet door on a prawn trawler.

David Feherty, 1993.

Sergio Garcia

Waggle boy.

Nickname bestowed on Garcia at the 2002 US Open, for his pre-shot routine of re-grips and hand twitches.

Todd Hamilton

Tex Harbinger? Tam Haematoma? … an absolute nonentity ruined a classic showdown yet again.

Matthew Norman in the *Evening Standard*, 19 July 2004, after US journeyman golfer Todd Hamilton won the 2004 Open.

Colin Montgomerie

He has a face like a warthog that's been stung by a wasp.

David Feherty on the best Scottish golfer never to have won a major.

Trevino on Trevino

If my IQ had been two points lower, I'd have been a plant somewhere.
Lee Trevino, US golfer.

I was twenty before I realised that Manual Labour wasn't a Mexican.
Lee Trevino.

Greg Norman

After he lost to Norman in a playoff for the World Matchplay:

I played crap, he played crap. He just out-crapped me.
Wayne Grady, 1990.

The American players have a new name for 'The Great White Shark'. Greg Norman is referred to as 'The Carp'.
Guy Hodgson in the *Independent on Sunday*, 1999.

Arnold Palmer

One of the reasons Arnie [Arnold Palmer] is playing so well is that, before each tee shot, his wife takes out his balls and kisses them.
Anon. US TV commentator.

Justin Rose

THE ROSE AND FALL OF JUSTIN

Sun headline, 9 July 2004 as an out-of-form Rose failed to qualify for the 2004 Open.

Lee Westwood

The world of golf was this week rocked by the news that Lee Westwood, one of the game's greatest pie-eaters, had gone on a diet.

'Backpages' in the *Guardian*, 11 May 2004.

I've found I can eat the foods I enjoy without the consequences. I particularly like the cottage pies, sausages and Swedish Style Balls.

Lee Westwood on the benefits of the mycoprotein meat substitute Quorn, with whose makers he signed an advertising contract in 2004; quoted in the *Guardian*, 11 May 2004.

Tiger Woods

I don't know. I've never played there.

Sandy Lyle, response when asked his opinion of Tiger Woods, 1992.

TIGER WOODS PLAYS WITH HIS OWN BALLS, NIKE SAYS

Newspaper headline.

The Ryder Cup

BIG MOUTH YANKS GET THEIR OWN BUTTS KICKED
Headline in the *Daily Star* after Europe retained the Ryder Cup following a tie, 1989.

The only thing that scares me is the Americans' dress sense.
Mark James, before the 1993 Ryder Cup.

Italy cost us two world wars. Now they have cost us the Ryder Cup.
Anon. German spectator, 1993 after Constantino Rocca lost his singles match at the Ryder Cup.

The most disgusting thing I've ever seen.
Sam Torrance on the notorious incident during the 1999 Ryder Cup at Brookline, Massachusetts when American players, wives, girlfriends, caddies and spectators prematurely rushed out to engulf US golfer Justin Leonard after his huge putt on the 17th green gave the USA the strong likelihood (but not yet absolute certainty) of victory. Leonard's opponent, Spain's José Maria Olazabal, had to wait for the celebrations to end before attempting a 25-foot putt to keep Europe's hopes alive. He missed.

Let us be painfully honest about it. Yes, they are repulsive people, charmless, rude, cocky, mercenary, humourless, ugly, full of nauseatingly fake religiosity, and as odious in victory as they are unsporting in defeat.
Matthew Norman gets steamed up in the *Evening Standard* over the same incident.

There are 150 people here, nobody saw it, nobody
heard it – it wouldn't happen to fucking Tiger
Woods.

Journeyman English golfer Gary Evans bemoans the loss of his ball in thick
rough at the 17th hole of the 2002 Open at Muirfield. Evans finished on five
under par after his final round, only one shot behind the four players who
appeared in the play-off for the title, which was eventually won by Ernie Els.
Woods ended six strokes behind the leaders after a third round 81 in
horrendous weather; quoted in the *Guardian*, 22 July 2002.

■ GOLF COMMENTATORS
(mainly Peter Alliss)

Seve Ballesteros makes Manuel sound like
A.J.P. Taylor giving a scintillating TV lecture
and Ken Brown could stun a charging rhino with
two syllables.

Matthew Norman on BBC TV's Open coverage, in the *Evening Standard*,
19 July 2004.

It would be an act of unimaginable masochism to
plough through a tape of Alliss commentary.

Marina Hyde in the *Guardian*, April 2004, on the golfer-turned-perennial-
BBC-TV- commentator.

The Peter Alliss tendency (those stringback,
driving glove-clad dullards who yearn for the
return of National Service) ... these tiresome
old farts.

Matthew Norman in the *Evening Standard*, 26 April 2004.

Alliss in Blunderland.

Matthew Norman in the *Evening Standard*, 12 July 2004.

The Socrates of the snug bar.

Matthew Norman on Peter Alliss in the *Evening Standard*, 12 July 2004.

Oops! Fannies and 69s

Ballesteros felt much better today after a 69.
US TV commentator Steve Ryder, at the US Masters.

Some weeks Nick likes to use Fanny, other weeks he prefers to do it by himself.
Ken Brown, TV commentator, on Nick Faldo and his caddy Fanny Sunneson lining up shots at the Scottish Open.

How some blazer-wearing, Lexus-driving oaf has failed to invite [Justin Rose] to the tournament [the Open] I do not ... wish to hear. But if there is any way of blaming Peter Alliss, however vague the link and however long it takes, I swear I'll find it.

Matthew Norman in the *Evening Standard*, 5 July 2004.

Dementia Pugilistica

The Ignoble Art of Boxing

To hell with the Queen of Marksbury.

Pierre Bouchard, 1973.

I now find the whole subject of professional boxing disgusting. Except for the fighters, you're talking about human scum, nothing more. Professional boxing is utterly immoral. It's not capable of reformation. You'll never clean it up. Mud can never be clean.

Howard Cosell, US commentator, 1982.

And now over to ringside, where Harry Commentator is your carpenter.

Anonymous BBC TV announcer, introducing commentator Harry Carpenter.

Probably the greatest of all arguments for banning boxing is the audience it attracts. No young people … Few blacks (outside the ring). No sentient girls, only middle-aged bits of fluff who look like Miss TV Times 1957. The noise that comes from their wretched throats indicates that, with a boxing crowd, brain damage is also in the head of the beholder.

Juile Burchill, *Damaged Gods* (1986).

Boxing is the only racket where you're almost guaranteed to end up as a bum.

Rocky Graziano, US middleweight boxer.

I got my brain shook, my money took, and my name in the undertaker's book.

Joe Frazier, US heavyweight boxer, in *The Times*, 31 December 1999.

Sure there have been injuries and deaths in boxing, but none of them serious.

Alan Minter, British boxer.

■ THE BOXERS

Muhammad Ali

He stings like a bee, but lives like a W.A.S.P.
Eamonn Andrews, 1972.

Now, quitting on his stool, he was a fallen, faded, jaded idol. He was, after all, fat and middle-aged like the rest of us.
Frank Keating on Ali's loss to Larry Holmes, 1980, in *Long Days, Long Nights*.

He now floats like an anchor, stings like a moth.
Ray Gandolfo, 1982, on the 39-year-old former champion.

Frank Bruno

Bruno still sounds like another British heavyweight, reminding us of Dorothy Parker's line: 'If all the British heavyweights were laid end to end, we wouldn't be surprised.'
Ring magazine.

BONKERS BRUNO LOCKED UP
Sun headline after Frank Bruno was sectioned under Britain's Mental Health Act, September 2003.

Bruno has a chin of such pure Waterford crystal, it gives rise to the old adage that people who live in glass jaws shouldn't throw punches. The biggest danger in fighting Bruno is that you might get hit by flying glass.

Jim Murray in the *Los Angeles Times*, 1996.

Joe Bugner

Jesus Christ, 60 per cent of all the Aussies I know think Joe Bugner is something you find up the Queensland Premier's nose.

The *New Australasian Express* on the Briton-turned-Aussie, 1987.

Henry Cooper

His potatoes kept getting cut eyes.

Reg Gutteridge, in *The Big Punchers*, explains why Our 'Enery gave up being a greengrocer.

'Jumbo' Cummings

'Jumbo' Cummings, a name that sounds like an elephant ejaculating.

Rory McGrath on the US heavyweight, *They Think it's All Over*, BBC TV, 1995.

Chris Eubank

Chris Eubank lost his recent comeback fight on points … the main one being that he's a total git.

Nick Hancock, *They Think It's All Over*, BBC TV, 1995.

'Ith time to thtop,' pugilitht Chris Eubank announces he is to quit the ring at age 29.

Total Sport, 1995.

Were you as surprised as we all were when he came from behind and licked you in the ring?

Mrs Merton to a bemused Eubank, following his defeat by Steve Collins, *The Mrs Merton Show*, BBC TV, 1995.

George Foreman

I'm going to beat your Christian ass, you white flag-waving son of a bitch!

Muhammad Ali taunts Foreman.

Some people say George is as fit as a fiddle, but I think he looks more like a cello.

US trainer Lou Duva on the veteran boxer's appearance, 1990.

He's a got a nutritionist, and I've got room service!

Foreman compares his diet with Evander Holyfield's.

Julius Francis

… the well-respected professional punchbag, Julius Francis.

Matthew Norman in the *Evening Standard* 10 May 2004.

Joe Frazier

He's so ugly they ought to donate his face to the US Bureau of Wildlife.

Muhammad Ali on his heavyweight rival, 1971.

Audley Harrison

Don't make me laugh! It's the WBF belt – I heard they are giving them away with five litres of petrol down at Texaco.

Herbie Hide on hearing that Harrison had won the world WBF heavyweight title; quoted on bbc.co.uk.

I've sparred with Harrison and I knocked him about. Basically he's fat, can't fight and can't knock anyone out, he's not strong enough to smash an egg with a baseball bat.

Hide on Harrison, again; quoted on bbc.co.uk.

Audley, lest it escape you, is a world heavyweight champion, holding the coveted belt of the WBF (World Boxing Fraudsters) ... perhaps Frank [Warren] would adjudicate as to where, in the pantheon of heavyweight titles the WBF ranks compared with the IBO (International Boxing Obesity) crown, held by Bernard Manning, and the vacant ICBM (Inter Continental Ballistic Muppet) belt, to be contested shortly by Chris Moyles and Jo Brand.

Matthew Norman in the *Evening Standard* 10 May 2004.

Larry Holmes

Larry has the dexterity to put both feet in his mouth.

Larry Merchant, US commentator.

Jake LaMotta

Me and Jake LaMotta grew up in the same neighbourhood. You wanna know how popular Jake was? When we played hide-and-seek, nobody ever looked for LaMotta.

US welterweight and middleweight boxer Rocky Graziano.

Lennox Lewis

Lennox Lewis, I'm coming for you man. My style is impetuous. My defense is impregnable, and I'm just ferocious. I want your heart. I want to eat his children. Praise be to Allah!

Mike Tyson.

Prince Naseem Hamed

Q: What sporting event would you pay most to watch?

A: Someone absolutely mashing Prince Naseem Hamed.

Leeds United footballer David Hopkin, in a *Sun* questionnaire, 1997.

Ali v. Liston — The verbal sparring

Isn't he ugly? He's too ugly to be the world's champ!
The world's champ should be pretty like me!
Muhammad Ali, before his 1964 fight with Liston.

Sonny Liston's so ugly that when he cries the tears run
down the back of his head.
Ali, before the same fight.

Here I predict Sonny Liston's dismemberment, I'll hit
him so hard he'll wonder where October–November
went.
Ali, at the weigh-in with Liston.

Sonny Liston would rather be dropped in the middle of
Vietnam with a peashooter 'fore he'd fight me again.
Ali, after defeating Liston.

Ernie Terrell

You're an Uncle Tom nigger and you're gonna get
your ass whipped.
Muhammad Ali makes a promise which he then kept.

Ali v. Patterson — The verbal sparring

I'll beat Floyd Patterson so bad he'll need a shoehorn to get his hat on.
Muhammad Ali before his fight with Floyd Patterson, October 1965.

Cassius Clay is disgracing himself and the Negro race … The image of a Black Muslim as the world heavyweight champion disgraces the sport and the nation. Cassius Clay must be beaten and the Black Muslim scourge removed from boxing.
Floyd Patterson, in *Sports Illustrated*, October 1965. Patterson had also claimed that it was his duty 'as a Catholic' to win back the world heavyweight title from the Muslim Ali.

… he's a deaf dumb so-called Negro who needs a spanking. I plan to punish him for the things he said; cause him pain … The little old pork-chop eater don't have a chance.
Ali's reply to Patterson. The black tennis player Arthur Ashe said of Ali's remark, 'No black athlete had ever publicly spoken so disparagingly to another black athlete.' Ali humiliated Patterson when they met in the ring, dragging out the fight to the 12th round and allowing Patterson to recover from his pummelling, then taunting him by saying, 'Come on, white America!'

Rick Thornberry

A poor bum whose head should be used to keep doors from slamming on a windy day.

Anthony Mundine, US boxer, on his next opponent. He was right.

Mike Tyson

After boxing, I would think Mike will resort to what he was doing when he was growing up – robbing people.

Tommy Brooks, Iron Mike's former trainer.

[He] called me a 'rapist' and a 'recluse'. I'm not a recluse.

Tyson objects to being insulted.

Mike Tyson's not all that bad. If you dig real deep, dig, dig, dig, dig, dig, deep, deep, go all the way to China … I'm sure you'll find there's a nice guy in there.

George Foreman.

Mike Tyson has recently found Islam, so his next fight could be a Ramadan-a-Ding-Dong affair.

Rory Bremner, 1995.

Heavyweight chomp

A BAD BITE FOR BOXING
The *News & Observer*, Raleigh.

DID TYSON BITE OFF MORE THAN HE CAN CHEW? TIME WILL TELL
The *Salt Lake Tribune*.

FROM CHAMP TO CHOMP
The *Herald-Sun*, Durham, North Carolina.

IRON MIKE GOES DOWN BITING
The *Sunday Oklahoman*.

PAY PER CHEW
Philadelphia Daily News.

SUCKER MUNCH
The *Sun*.

LOBE BLOW FOR BOXING
The *Tennessean*.

Selected headlines after Tyson bit off part of Evander Holyfield's ear during a world title bout, 1997.

■ PROMOTERS
la scum de la scum

All boxers are prostitutes and all promoters are pimps.
Larry Holmes, US heavyweight.

Never in the ring of human conflict have so few taken so much from so many.
Saoul Mamby, US super-lightweight boxer.

Bob Arum

'But Bob, yesterday you told me the exact opposite.'
'I know. Today I'm telling the truth. Yesterday I was lying.'
Newsweek columnist Bob Waters, recalling a conversation with Arum.

When Bob Arum pats you on the back, he's just looking for a spot to stick the knife.
Cus D'Amato, US trainer.

I advise all the fighters in the world, black or white, to stay away from the fucker.
Larry Holmes.

Bob Arum is one of the worst people in the Western Hemisphere. I don't know the Eastern Hemisphere very well, but I suspect he'd be one of the worst people there, too.

Cus D'Amato.

Don King is like everything else in boxing. He's a liar, a thief, a murderer and a racketeer. And a con man. But there ain't nobody as bad as Bob Arum. That New York City Jew lawyer will make you hate city folks, Jews, and lawyers in the same day.

Randall 'Tex' Cobb, US boxer and film actor.

Don King

Since then we've changed the locks.

James McNulty, Mayor of Scranton, Pennsylvania, recalling the day in 1975 when Don King was presented with the Keys of the City.

This is the lying, thieving mother who cut me to $500,000.

Randall 'Tex' Cobb introduces Don King to a press conference after the Cobb–Holmes fight, 1982; King had cut Cobb's purse because the fight was a commercial flop.

Don King is a liar and a thief, the greediest bastard I've ever known.

Richie Giachetti, in *Black Lights*. Oddly, he added: 'If I was a fighter and I needed a promoter, who would I take? Don King. He's the best.'

Don King is a damn sleazebag. King is nothing but a strong-arm man. He has taken his gangsterism and put it into boxing.

Dan Duva, rival US promoter, quoted in the *New York Daily News*, 1986.

You put your head in a noose when you sign with Don King.

Mitch Green, US heavyweight, in *The City Sun*, 1987.

I tried to stay away from King. You can't do it. It's like staying away from taxes. Sooner or later, he'll get you.

Pinklon Thomas, former WBC heavyweight champion.

I still love Don, he's a great guy. But he's evil, and he steals people's money.

Mike Tyson, quoted in the *Daily Telegraph*, 18 January 1999.

Don King is one of the great humanitarians of our time. He has risen above that great term, prejudice. He has screwed everyone he has ever been around. Hog, dog, or frog, it don't matter to Don. If you got a quarter, he wants the first twenty-six cents.

Randall 'Tex' Cobb, in *Ring* magazine.

Isolationist Sports of America

AMERICAN FOOTBALL
armour-plated rugby

American football makes rugby look like a
Tupperware party.
Sue Lawley, broadcaster, 1985.

Football is a beastly game played by beasts.
Henry Blaha, 1972.

I will not permit thirty men to travel four hundred
miles to agitate a bag of wind.
Andrew Dickson White, president of Cornell University from 1867 to 1885, on
not allowing the Cornell football team to play a match in Michigan.

Anybody who watches three games of football in a
row should be declared brain dead.
Erma Bombeck, US journalist.

College football is a sport that bears the same
relation to education that bullfighting does to
agriculture.
Elbert Hubbard, US journalist and author.

Football combines the two worst features of American life: it is violence punctuated by committee meetings.

George Will, US educationalist, *The Pursuit of Happiness and Other Sobering Thoughts* (1978).

Football is the only game you come into with a semblance of intelligence and end up a babbling moron.

Mike Adamle, footballer and commentator.

One of the great disappointments of a football game is that the cheerleaders never seem to get injured.

New York Tribune.

Big and dumb: the players

He doesn't know the meaning of the word fear. Of course, there are lots of words he doesn't know the meaning of.

Sid Gilman, American football coach, 1963, on the typical player.

There's this interior linesman who's big as a gorilla and strong as a gorilla. If he was smart as a gorilla he'd be fine.

Dan Millman, coach, 1972.

Terry Bradshaw couldn't spell cat, if you spotted him the 'C' and the 'A'.

Thomas 'Hollywood' Henderson, player for Dallas Cowboys.

Most football teams are temperamental. That's 90% temper and 10% mental.

Doug Plank.

Mark Gastineau has got an IQ of about room temperature.

Dan Hampton.

Physically, Alonzo Spellman is a world beater. Mentally, he's an egg beater.

Matt Elliott.

The only qualifications for a lineman are to be big and dumb. To be a back you only have to be dumb.

Knute Rockne, American football coach, aka 'The Gipper'.

Football kickers are like taxi cabs. You can always go out and hire another one.

Buddy Ryan, US coach, 1986.

■ BASKETBALL
therapy for tall people

The game is too long, the season is too long … and the players are too long.

Jack Dolph, basketball manager, 1973.

You are a whore and a pimp.

Bobby Knight, basketball coach at Indiana University, to US columnist John Feinstein. Feinstein commented: 'I wish he'd just make up his mind, so I know how to dress.'

Basketball … is staying in after school in your underwear.

Ring Lardner, US humorist, quoted in the film *Drive He Said* (1971).

I miss America. I miss crime and murder. I miss Philadelphia. There hasn't been a brutal stabbing or anything here the last 24 hours. I've missed it.

Charles Barkley, US basketball player, at the 1992 Barcelona Olympics.

… the sole qualification hurdle between a promising basketball player and an Ivy League scholarship is the ability to tie a shoelace.

Matthew Norman in the *Evening Standard* 1 March 2004.

■ BASEBALL
rounders with hype

Baseball is the favourite American sport because it's so slow. Any idiot can follow it. And just about any idiot can play it.
Gore Vidal, US novelist and essayist.

There is nothing remarkable about throwing or catching or hitting a ball. Jugglers in Yugoslavia do it better.
Jim Murray in the *Los Angeles Times*, 1974.

The underprivileged people of America play some strange game with a bat that looks like an overgrown rolling-pin.
Fred Trueman, English cricketer.

What do you have when you've got an agent buried up to his neck in sand? Not enough sand.
Pat Williams, US baseball player.

In the great department store of life, baseball is the toy department.
Anon. US sports commentator, quoted in the *Independent*, 28 September 1991.

George Steinbrenner

Working for Genghis Khan

Seeing as how none of us has ever worked for Genghis Khan, how does it feel to work for George Steinbrenner?

TV interviewer Ted Dawson asks Yankees manager Gene Michael (1980 and 1982) about George Steinbrenner, owner of the New York Yankees since 1973 (and counting).

The United Nations has universally denounced Saddam Hussein, the Europeans are calling him the Hitler of the Middle East, and the Arabs are calling him the Butcher of Baghdad. The Americans, though, are calling him the Steinbrenner of Iraq – and you can't get much worse than that.

Jay Leno, in the buildup to the Gulf War of 1990.

I have lots of reasons to hate baseball. For one it's dull. Nothing happens. Watching baseball is like going to a lecture by a member of the Slow … Talkers … of … America. It's like turning on the TV … when the cable is out.

Jeff Jarvis, *Entertainment Weekly*, 1990.

Spoiled, 20-year-old millionaire boys with pornographic minds, sixth-grade vocabularies, and good throwing arms.
Andrea Peyser in the *New York Post*, on baseball players.

I don't know why ballplayers like to moon. Maybe it's the only way some of them can figure out how to express themselves.
Former player Jay Johnstone.

I don't think I can be expected to take seriously any game which takes less than three days to reach its conclusion.
Tom Stoppard, English playwright, quoted in the *Guardian*, 24 December 1984.

Managing a baseball team is like trying to make chicken salad out of chicken shit.

Joe Kuhel.

Other Sports

(Mostly Dull Ones)

■ ATHLETICS

The decathlon is nine Mickey Mouse events and a slow 1500 metres.

Steve Ovett ... British 1500 metres specialist.

I don't think the discus will ever attract any interest until they let us start throwing them at one another.

Al Oerter, US discus thrower.

Italian men and Russian women don't shave before a race.

Eddie Ottoz.

No way has been found to stop long-jump commentaries sounding like naughty stories after lights-out in the dorm – 'Ooooh! It's enormous. It was so long!'

Russell Davies in *The Sunday Times*.

If you want to know what you'll look like after ten years, look in the mirror after you've run a marathon.

Jeff Scaff.

Athens 2004

A sickly spectacle at the best of times, in these worst of times the prospect of sub-Pepsi ad arrangement of winsome Hellenic infants singing of the brotherhood of nations has me slipping the phrase "sickbags + extra absorbent" into the Google search engine.

Matthew Norman on the prospect of watching an Olympic opening ceremony during a time of conflict in the Middle East, in the *Evening Standard* 10 May 2004.

A new sport has been introduced in Athens this summer. It takes place over four stages: denial, excuses, panic and backlash and the hosts are gold medal-winners at it.

Martin Samuel, *The Times*, 18 August. See Drugs on page 299.

The *Guardian* would not let me go to Athens because someone has to stay at home to make sarcastic remarks about Clare Balding's hairstyle ... practical for standing around in the searing heat but rather severe, with a strictly regimented side parting, and the rest of the hair swept tightly across the head. Very Prisoner Cell Block H.

Guardian journalist Martin Kelner on BBC Olympics commentator Clare Balding, 19 August 2004.

Linford Christie

Linford Christie, the generously beloined sprint supremo.

Punch magazine.

There's nothing new you can say about Linford Christie – except he's slow and has got a small penis.

Nick Hancock *They Think It's All Over*, BBC TV, 1995.

Sebastian Coe

Seb Coe is a Yorkshireman. So he's a complete bastard and will do well in politics.

Daley Thompson, 1993, on Coe's move into Conservative politics.

Jonathan Edwards

… that creeping Jesus of the sandpit.

Matthew Norman in the *Evening Standard* 10 May 2004.

Maurice Greene

G.O.A.T.

Not an insult, in fact, but an immodest tattoo on the shoulder of the US sprinter known as the 'Kansas Cannonball', standing for Greatest Of All Time.

Can you really be heroic with a name like Maurice?

The *Guardian*: Olympics 2004, August 2004.

Drugs | Beware Greeks dodging tests

You have to be suspicious when you line up against girls with moustaches.
Maree Holland, 1983.

It should not have surprised anyone that Ben Johnson was using steroids. You don't go from 10.17 [seconds] to 9.83 on unleaded gas.
Jamie Astaphan on the steroid-taking Canadian sprinter, 1989.

American audiences love fairytales, but fairytales don't have ugly supporting cast lists which include C.J. Hunter (shotputting dope), Charlie Francis (Ben Johnson's coach) and Victor Conte (founder of BALCO indicted on steroid-related charges).
Ian Chadband in the *Evening Standard*, 12 July 2004.

BEWARE GREEKS DODGING TESTS
Richard Williams, headline to an article in the *Guardian*, 19 August 2004, about Kostas Kenteris, the Greek sprinter who failed to attend a drugs test before the 2004 Olympic Games. Kenteris, who raised eyebrows when he came from obscurity to win the 200-metres gold in Sydney, withdrew from the games following a bizarre incident in which he and his training partner Ekaterini Thanou were apparently involved in a motorbike accident.

Commentary classics

And the line-up for the final of the women's 400 metres hurdles includes three Russians, two East Germans, a Pole, a Swede and a Frenchman.
David Coleman, BBC TV.

Every time he opens his legs he shows his class.
Ron Pickering, BBC TV commentator, referring to Cuban runner Alberto Juantorena during the 1976 Montreal Olympics.

Zola Budd: so small, so waif-like, you literally can't see her. But there she is.
Alan Parry, BBC TV commentator, on the South African-turned Briton.

I hope the Romanian doesn't get through, because I can't pronounce her bloody name!
David Coleman thinks he is off air during an Olympic Games broadcast.

She's not Ben Johnson – but then who is?
David Coleman, BBC TV.

Linford Christie's got a habit of pulling it out when it matters most.
David Coleman, quoted in *The Times*, 'The Eye', 14 August 2004.

Michael Johnson

If [Johnson] ran with his fingers up his bum he could still run 42 seconds.

Roger Black on the 400 metres US runner, 1995.

Marion Jones and C.J. Hunter

Beauty and the Beast.

Journalists' nickname for the US sprinter Marion Jones and her big, drug-banned, shot-putting former partner C.J. Hunter.

Carl Lewis

There's going to be some serious celebrating when Carl gets beaten.

Larry Myricks on the two-times Olympic 100 metres champion, 1984.

I wouldn't be surprised if one day Carl's halo slipped and choked him.

British sprinter Allan Wells, referring in 1989 to Lewis's wholesome public image.

When Lewis briefly sported a ponytail:

He looks like the love child of Grace Jones and Paul Revere.

Tony Kornheiser in the *Washington Post*, 1990.

Steve Ovett

Pity Steve Ovett didn't show up. Then we could have the good, the bald and the ugly.

Daley Thompson, 1980, after a photocall with fellow Olympic gold medallist Duncan Goodhew.

Paula Radcliffe

… it is as if, with each record-breaking stride, she is being poked in the back of the head with a ruler.

The *Observer Sport Monthly* is irritated by Paula's nodding head, May 2004.

There's a touch of Julie Andrews syndrome. Her deal with nicey-nicey Cadbury's sums it up: fit but square.

The *Guardian*: Olympics 2004, August 2004.

… the poster-girl for our true national sport of self-flagellation.

Marina Hyde in the *Guardian*, 25 August 2004. Paula Radcliffe, favourite for the Olympic marathon in Athens, made a tearful public apology for unexpectedly dropping out of the race after running 20 miles in searing heat.

■ DARTS
finely-tuned lard

I was watching Sumo wrestling on the television for two hours before I realised it was darts.

Hattie Hayridge, British comedienne, 1989.

Bald and badly tattooed, with skin the colour of wallpaper paste, Hankey will look tonight, under the unforgiving lights of television, as if he were two decades older than his 32 years. Now, though, bent over his beer, he looks beautiful – born to the bar, one hand on his head and one on his Harp, lost in concentration, a Rodin sculpture: The Drinker.

Steve Rushin on British player Ted Hankey in *Sports Illustrated*, 2 April 2001.

To be perfectly honest with you, I think it was the introduction of the Breathalyzer.

Darts commentator Tony Green, explains why darts has declined in popularity, in *Sports Illustrated*, 2 April 2001.

I've been described as fat, boozy and toothless. That's pretty accurate.

'Jocky' Wilson, 1982.

Jocky Wilson is the minimum of mass into which a human being can be contracted.

Nancy Banks-Smith in the *Guardian*, 1990.

Andy The 30-stone Viking athlete

You only have to take one look at Andy Fordham ... to see that darts still ain't a sport. Fordham is a 30-stone beer monster with forearms the size of a lady's thigh. He is self-evidently not an athlete ... God only knows what his training regime involves – lifting pints of beer all day by the looks of it.

Duleep Alliraja, *Spiked Online*, 16 January 2004.

'I tell people these trainers aren't for show, I'm an athlete,' growled The Viking. In fact Fordham wears trainers on the oche – and he is the only darts player allowed to do so – because his feet swell up during long matches (a lovely thought).

Duleep Alliraja, *Spiked Online*, 16 January 2004.

■ FORMULA ONE
boredom and terror

Racing is 99 per cent boredom and one per cent terror.

Geoff Brabham.

The point of Formula One is to export lung cancer and emphysema to the impressionable youth of the Far East and so long as it succeeds in that noble aim, the pressure to be exciting is resistable.

Matthew Norman in the *Evening Standard*, 12 July 2004.

Grand Prix motor racing is like *Punch*. It is never as good as it was.

Maxwell Boyd.

Motor racing's less of a sport these days than a commercial break doing 150 mph.

Peter Dunne in the *Independent on Sunday*, 1992.

Grand prix? Grand Bore.

The Times, 5 July 2004, bemoans the tedium of a sport dominated by Michael Schumacher and Ferrari.

James Hunt

Hunt the Shunt.

Nickname given to the flamboyant 1976 world champion in his volatile
younger days.

'Was it out of tension, James?'
'No, probably too much foie gras and champagne
last night.'

Question to and reply from Hunt after he had vomited in the cockpit on the
last lap of a victorious run in the French Grand Prix, quoted in the
Independent, 10 July 2004.

Murray ... **Missing you already**

Murray sounds like a blindfolded man riding a unicycle on the rim of the pit of doom.
Clive James on Murray Walker.

Even in moments of tranquillity, Murray Walker sounds like a man whose trousers are on fire.
Clive James again.

Unless I'm very much mistaken ... I am very much mistaken!

Mansell is slowing it down, taking it easy ... Oh no he isn't! It's a lap record.

I imagine that the conditions in those cars today are totally unimaginable.

Patrick Tambay's hopes, which were nil before, are absolutely zero now.

Do my eyes deceive me, or is Senna's car sounding a bit rough?
Murray Walker, BBC TV.

Nigel Mansell

Nigel Mansell is someone with about as much charisma as a damp spark plug.

Alan Hubbard, the *Observer,* on British Formula One ace Nigel Mansell, 1992.

He should have 'Who Dares Whines' embroidered on his overalls.

Simon Barnes in *The Times*, 1993.

Nigel Mansell is the only man who goes to Nick Faldo for charisma lessons.

Nick Hancock, *They Think It's All Over*, BBC TV, 1995.

Alain Prost

On receiving an OBE from the British government:
When I drove for British teams they called me 'The Tadpole' because I was too small to be a frog.

Alain Prost, 1994.

Michael Schumacher

… that long-faced German troll.

Matthew Norman in the *Evening Standard*, 1 March 2004.

He's killing the sport single-handedly, isn't he?

Question asked by Tom Clarkson in *The Times*, 5 July 2004, in the light of another Formula One season dominated by Schumacher and Ferrari.

Feuding Scotsmen

If I see him I'll wrap his kilt round his head.
Formula One boss Bernie Ecclestone on Jackie Stewart,
during the pair's war of words over the future of the
Silverstone track, quoted in the *Guardian*, 10 July 2004.
Stewart responded: 'When I read that quote I was actually
wearing grey flannel trousers.'

Add up the manner of his nine victories in ten
races this season and it would be difficult to
conjure up a single memorable moment.
Kevin Eason in *The Times*, 5 July 2004.

Ralf Schumacher

What does it feel like being rammed up the backside by Barrichello?
James Allen puts the question to Ralf Schumacher.

■ HORSE RACING
anorexic dwarves in bright colours

I have no intention of watching undersized Englishmen perched on horses with matchstick legs race along courses planned to amuse Nell Gwynn.
Gilbert Harding.

My horse was in the lead, coming down the home stretch, but the caddie fell off.
Samuel Goldwyn.

Jockey (Flat): An anorexic dwarf in bright colours who drives a large car with cushions on the seat and blocks on the pedals.
Jockey (Jump): Punch-drunk, nobbly, occasionally hot-headed individual who must be as stupid as he looks to take 100 times as many risks as the flat counterpart for one hundredth of the rewards.
Julian Seaman in *Turfed Out* (1988).

There are three racecourses beginning with the letter F – namely Fontwell, Folkestone and effing Plumpton.
Attributed to Fred Winter.

From the commentary box

This is really a lovely horse. I once rode her mother.
Ted Walsh, commentator.

And there's the unmistakable figure of Joe Mercer ...
or is it Lester Piggott?
Brough Scott, ITV, 1981.

The racecourse is as level as a billard ball.
John Francome, Channel Four, 1995.

My word, look at that magnificent erection!
Brough Scott again, on the new stand at the Doncaster
course.

She's about as cuddly as a dead hedgehog. The
Alsatians in her yard would go about in pairs for
protection.
Jockey John Francombe on racehorse trainer Jenny Pitman, in *The Times*,
31 December 1999.

He has a face like a well-kept grave.

Jack Leach on Lester Piggott.

John McCririck ... looking like a hedge dragged
through a man backwards.
The *Sunday Express* on the racing commentator, 1994.

Not-so-Royal Ascot ...

Ascot in the last five years has slumped from a
My Fair Lady spectacle into a vulgar and tatty farce.
Jean Rook in the *Daily Express*, 1983.

Willie Carson, riding his 180th winner of the
season, spent the last two furlongs looking over
one shoulder then another, even between his legs,
but there was nothing there to worry him.
Sporting Life.

They usually have four or five dreams a night about coming from different positions.

Willie Carson tells BBC TV's Claire Balding how jockeys prepare for a big race.

If I never hear another interview with the
terminally irritating Frankie Dettori I will not feel
my life to be significantly impoverished.
Martin Kelner in the *Guardian*, 22 June 2004.

■ ROWING
(mainly the Boat Race)

Don't you think it's going to be rather wet for the horses?

Spike Milligan, on being told the route of the Boat Race.

The Oxford–Cambridge boat race would be much more attractive if the boats were allowed to ram each other.

Miles Kington, quoted in the *Guinness Book of Humorous Sports Quotes* (1996).

Tens of millions of people watch the Boat Race and in an internet poll 25% say they want Cambridge to win, 27% says they want Oxford to win and 48% say they don't care who wins so long as the commentator makes a hilarious double-entendre involving loose rowlocks, pulling oars, strokes and catching crabs.

Harry Pearson, 'What won't happen this week' (Sunday), in the *Guardian*, 22 March 2004.

… an activity that might have been designed for insomniacs with sleeping-pill allergies.

Matthew Norman, 'A Sinking Feeling as Beeb loses Boat Race', in the *Evening Standard*, 1 March 2004.

Abusing the cox

And the victorious crew celebrate in the traditional manner – dipping their cox into the Thames.
Harry Pearson in the *Guardian*, 22 March 2004.

Ah! Isn't that nice, the wife of the Cambridge President is kissing the cox of the Oxford crew.
Harry Carpenter, BBC TV commentator, during the 1977 Boat Race.

If you want to see muscle-bound thickies doing strange things with wooden paddles, and London's lively fetish scene isn't your ticket, go down to the towpath.
Matthew Norman in the *Evening Standard*, 1 March 2004.

Anyone who sees me go anywhere near a boat again, ever, you've got my permission to shoot me.

Steve Redgrave after winning his fourth Olympic gold medal, Atlanta 1996. In 1997 he reversed the decision and went on to win a fifth gold at the 2000 Sydney Games, and a knighthood thereafter.

■ SKIING AND SKI-JUMPING
sliding into debt

Skis are a pair of long, thin flexible runners that permit a skier to slide across the snow and into debt.

Henry Beard *Skiing* (1989).

Eddie the Eagle

Mr Edwards' Olympic performance was the equivalent of a first-ball duck in a test match, two own goals in a Wembley cup final, or a first round 168 in the Open Championship.

Ian Wooldridge in the *Daily Mail*, 1988.

We have thousands of Eddie Edwards in Norway, but we never let them jump.

Torbjorn Yggeseth, 1988.

■ SNOOKER
chess with balls

Billiards is very similar to snooker, except that there are only three balls and no-one watches it.

Steve Davis, 1988.

Steve Davis

I suppose the charisma bypass operation was a big disappointment in my life.

Steve Davis, world snooker champion, caricatured on ITV's *Spitting Image* as Steve 'Interesting' Davis.

Quinten Hann

He reached new levels of stupidity even by his own cretinous standards … the Aussie slob.

John Rawling on Australian snooker player Quinten Hann; 'Boorish O'Sullivan needs a rocket to get his game in order' in the *Guardian* 20 April 2004.

Stephen Hendry

Stephen Hendry is the only man with a face that comes with free garlic bread.

Nick Hancock on Scotland's seven-times world snooker champion, *They Think It's All Over*, BBC TV, 1995.

Alex Higgins

Alex Higgins' autobiography is called *Alex Through the Looking Glass* ... Through the Plate Glass Window would have been more appropriate.

Nick Hancock *They Think It's All Over*, 1995.

Back in Belfast, someone threw Alex a petrol bomb and he drank it.

Frank Carson.

From the commentary box

Fred Davis, the doyen of snooker, now 67 years of age and too old to get his leg over, prefers to use his left hand.

'Whispering' Ted Lowe, BBC2 commentary.

Griffiths is snookered on the brown, which, for those of you watching in black and white, is the ball directly behind the pink.

Ted Lowe, BBC2 commentary.

And that's the third time he's missed his waistcoat pocket with the chalk.

Ted Lowe, BBC2 commentary.

The most frightening experience I have ever had in sport was getting into a lift with Alex Higgins. He did nothing. He said nothing. Yet there was an aura surrounding him ... that sent shivers up the spine.

Stephen Bierley in the *Guardian* 4 May 2004. Bierley continued: 'He was not a nice man, he was given to gratuitous violence and threats.'

What about that Alex Higgins? ... He's off his tits. All that money and fame and shit and he's blown the lot. What a way to go. I hope that happens to me. One big fucking blow-out. Top.

Oasis singer Liam Gallagher.

Ronnie O'Sullivan

It is actually quite difficult to summon the desire for vengeance on a chap in a bow tie and hairband.

Sue Mott in the *Daily Telegraph*, 27 April 2004. On Ronnie O'Sullivan, who had drawn criticism for use of bad language at the World Snooker championships.

[His] wild looks and wilder behaviour suggest he may be the Gallagher brother Liam and Noel threw out of Oasis for being too unstable.

Matthew Norman in the *Evening Standard*, 26 April 2004.

The hurricanes and whirlwinds have blown out, and we are left with a rocket in an Alice band.

Stephen Bierley in the *Guardian*, 4 May 2004, on Ronnie 'Rocket' O'Sullivan, winner of the World Snooker Championship 2004.

Bill Werbeniuk

The Hoover from Vancouver.

Nickname bestowed for the Canadian's capacity for lager.

People say that because of a lady's shape, it isn't possible for them to play snooker well. That shape hasn't prevented Bill Werbeniuk earning a decent living.

Alison Fisher, 1986.

Jimmy White

I don't want to be disrespectful to my fellow-players but it's a joke how I keep losing to so many mugs.

Jimmy White, quoted by Stephen Bierley in the *Guardian* 4 May 2004.

Postscript That's never a sport!

Beach volleyball: **The only sport this resembles is the** *Sunday Sport*.

Dressage: **The riders wear top hats. Their mounts have their hair in plaits. Together they do the foxtrot. Remember that Echo and the Bunnymen song 'Bring on the Dancing Horses'? It made no sense and neither does this.**

Rhythmic gymnastics: **Adolescent girls the size of pixies, made up like the women on department store perfume counters, grinning like corpses while they wave a ribbon or bounce a ball.**

Synchronized diving: **Two svelte young men with hairless chests jump off a board and land in a swimming pool at the same time head first: it's not clever, it's not artistic: it's gravity.**

Synchronized swimming: **Women in silver swimming costumes waving their legs in the air to show tunes like Busby Berkeley, only with 50 times fewer people.**

Weightlifting: **They walk on, they lift something up, they walk off again. Why do they need to wear leotards? Removal men don't and they do exactly the same job.**

The *Guardian*: Olympics 2004, August 2004.